TABLE OF CONTENTS

SECTION ONE: ELECTRIC VEHICLE INNOVATIONS

SECTION TWO: ROBOTIC INNOVATIONS

SECTION THREE: SUSTAINABLE PRODUCT INNOVATIONS

SECTION FOUR: CONNECTIVITY INNOVATIONS

SECTION FIVE: ENVIRONMENTAL & ENERGY INNOVATIONS

SECTION SIX: TRAVEL INNOVATION

INTRODUCTION

The 2020's are destined to be a decade of disruptive innovation. Exponential new inventions and breakthrough developments are accelerating the emerging widespread use of electric and autonomous cars. A new world of intelligent, collaborative robotics is just beginning along with massive communications accessibility for all of us through 5G and 6G connectivity. Exciting new inventions are under development that will have a real impact on reversing global climate change. One of the hottest new innovation sectors is sustainable products that, for instance, are only powered by light. And, there are extraordinary new forms of travel modes like Google's Larry Page and Boeing's Wisk Aero flying car.

As a business journalist and licensed stock broker, I've written an investor's information source to the latest and most impactful new innovations. I've focused the book "Investing in Disruptive Innovations" on the six industrial segments where I'm tracking rapid global breakthroughs. The sectors are: electric vehicles, robotics, connectivity, climate change remedies, sustainable products and new travel modes.

For the savvy investor, my book provides news summaries on nearly 80 top, new inventions. The book is designed to serve as a take-off point for the reader to explore the innovation, do their own independent research and due diligence and then personally determine if it's an investment bet you'd like to make.

My co-author Maryanne Kane and I are journalists writing news summaries on breakthrough, global innovations with the level of market potential to track for the possibility of investment. The material provided is intended for research and information purposes and does not constitute advice or recommendations. Any products referenced or linked in the material are not endorsed.

I hope you enjoy reading the book as much as I enjoyed researching and writing it.

Thanks and best,

Ed Kane, Author of "Investing in Disruptive Innovations"

AUTHOR'S BIOGRAPHY

Ed Kane created and serves as Executive Producer of CEO Global Foresight. CGF is a national news, public affairs program on PBS focused on breakthrough innovations changing our lives for the better. He also created and served as Executive Producer of CEO Corner, a long-running CEO interview program on NECN. Ed is a licensed stock broker who worked for Smith Barney. He is the author of fourteen books on the latest innovations. Ed is a science graduate of the University of Pennsylvania. He is an avid researcher into the future of breakthrough innovation and its impact on humanity.

SECTION ONE: ELECTRIC VEHICLE INNOVATIONS

1. Electric Vehicle of Choice for the 2020's - Electric Bikes

Source: Electric Bikes in Traffic Stock Image

Big Selling Surge Forecast by Deloitte

The 2020's will be the decade of electric vehicles. But what may surprise you is that the biggest selling electric vehicle is going to be electric bikes not electric cars. Just between 2020 and 2023, 130 million electric bikes will be sold globally, according to Deloitte, the global consulting company. Deloitte also forecasts that the number of electric bikes on the road will outnumber other electric vehicles globally by the end of 2020. What they are forecasting is a strong sales surge for e-bikes

E-Bike Riding

It's been a slow sales climb for e-bikes particularly in the early years of the 2010's. For instance, in 2013, only 185,000 e-bikes were sold in the US. Since then, there have been seismic changes that include greater power, improved lithium ion batteries, greater tech and better pricing. Plus, a focus by global cities and nations to cut carbon emissions, reduce car traffic and go for zero emissions as soon as possible. That has ushered in a new era of electric bikes in big cities globally.

Need for New Infrastructure

To make the new e-bike travel market really flourish, there is a need for new infrastructure. Priorities are regulations to support networks of protected bike lanes for safe electric bike riding and also places to park and lock the e-bike for protection. It's the future of travel and it's riding up to your doorstep as an environmentally friendly means of transportation.

2. **VW & Tesla Accelerating EV Production to Meet Growing Global Demand**

Source: VW ID Crozz

Ahead of Electric Targets

Volkswagen announced in late December 2019 that it's way ahead of schedule in the production of electric vehicles. In fact, it's two years ahead of its targeted numbers. By the end of 2023, it will have produced 1 million electric vehicles. It expects to have produced 1.5 million EVs by 2025. These are important milestones for VW because the future of driving in the 2020's is accelerating toward EVs, These are vehicles that are all-electric with no emissions, green, clean and great for the global environment.

Tesla and China Synergies

Meanwhile, Tesla is reaching a landmark. The first delivery of its China-made Model 3 EV hit on December 30, 2019. The turnaround time on these EVs is incredibly fast. In fact, it's a record for a global automaker in China. Construction started on Tesla's first plant outside of the US, in Shanghai, China in January 2019. Vehicle production in the plant started in October and the first products were delivered on December 30, 2019. The price of the Model 3 is about $50,000.

China is World's Biggest EV Market

China is by far the world's biggest electric vehicle market with 1.3 million electric vehicles sold in 2018. Tesla is capitalizing on the China opportunity. In its new Shanghai facility, it hopes to produce 250,000 vehicles a year after they add in production of the Tesla Model Y. The Chinese government is supporting Tesla vehicle sales in China by exempting their models from purchase taxes. On its part, Tesla is smartly building a big customer base by establishing service centers and charging stations across China to provide substantive, "after-sales" services to its Chinese customers. These investments in EVs by VW and Tesla are worth watching by investors.

3. Revolutionary Approach to Building EV's: Israel's REE

Source: R3E

Engines in the Wheels to Increase Efficiencies and Cut Costs

REE, an Israeli start-up based in Tel Aviv, aims to reimagine the future of electric vehicles. They've developed potentially disruptive technology that enables a completely different way of building electric vehicles. They've created a flat and modular chassis. That allows all engine components to be put directly next to the wheels and below the body of the car. The design reduces weight and space and increases efficiencies. Essentially, the team has developed a new electro-mobility platform that works across models from powerful cars to 10 ton trucks.

Skateboard Chassis

REE calls it a skateboard chassis. The modular design puts the engine, suspension, steering, electronics, powertrain, brakes and other components right next to the wheels. This fundamentally changes the way cars are built. Furthermore the system is lightweight, with a gearbox that weighs 13 pounds instead of the standard 440 pounds.

Big Investors Wanted

REE has partnered with Mitsubishi and other leading automotive players on their technology. They are currently seeking investors to ramp up into mass industrial production. Their skateboard chassis allows manufacturers to design the car as they want it. And because the chassis is modular it can be used on a wide range of models, while cutting costs significantly.

4. Wall Street's $1.3 Billion Bet on EV Startup Rivian

Source: Rivian R1S SUV

Unique EV "Skateboard Technology" for Cars, Trucks, SUVs

The 2020's are going to be hot growth years for electric vehicles. Detroit-based EV startup Rivian at the end of 2019 closed on a $1.3 billion investment round led by T. Rowe Price. The Wall Street investors are joined by existing stakeholders Ford and Amazon.

Rivian's Differentiator: Unique Technology

Rivian's technological approach to electric vehicles is unique. It has a patented "skateboard" design. The skateboard is the chassis that bundles the electric motors, batteries and controls. Moreover, the skateboard design can accommodate a variety of models and body styles. That's just one of the unique aspects of Rivian that attracted Ford to invest $500 million in the startup company.

Big 2020 Development Plan

Rivan is currently valued at $5 to $7 billion. It previously raised $2.2 billion from investors. It plans to build its all electric pickup truck, the R1T, in late 2020, along with the R1S SUV. Also, Ford's all-electric Lincoln SUVs will be built on Rivian skateboards starting in 2022.

Accelerating Electric Vehicle Competition

In the global EV industry, Tesla is the strongest and most established player. But the $1.3 billion latest investment in Rivian places it as one of the industry's better financed players. In China and Europe, there's a tremendous push to bring EVs to market to meet toughening emissions standards. In the US, GM and Ford are pouring billions of dollars into EV development.

Wall Street and Amazon Betting on This

Amazon has invested $700 million in Rivian. And, it has ordered 100,000 electric delivery trucks to be built in 2022. T. Rowe Price says Rivian is pushing the innovation frontier forward with its "sustainable transport solutions for consumers and business".

Clearly, the electric vehicle sector and startup Rivian are emerging investment opportunities to watch for breakthrough global innovations for investors to explore.

5. World's 1st Electrified, Autonomous Hypercar

Source: Geneva Auto Show 2018

Rimac's C Two: World's Fastest Car

Croatian startup Rimac, with the financial backing of Porsche, Kia and Hyundai, has developed the world's first electrified, autonomous hypercar, the limited edition C Two. The vehicle was unveiled at the 2018 Geneva Auto Show as a concept close to production. It received great reviews and orders for the $2 million vehicle sold out in record time. The company is now closing in on delivering those orders by late 2020. Porsche has at least a 15%

investment stake in Rimac.

Loaded with Highly Advanced Technology: Electric and Level 4 Autonomous

The vehicle has four electric motors that deliver 1,914 horsepower. It may be the world's fastest car. Rimac says in 1.85 seconds it accelerates from 0 to 60 mph. To go autonomous, the technology suite includes 6 radar sensors, lidar, 8 cameras, 12 ultrasonic sensors. All of that technology delivers Level 4, hands free driving. The technology for Level 4 driving generates 8 terabytes per hour. Rimac CEO Mate Rimac says he and his engineering team used detailed computer simulations to design the car.

17 Prototypes and Back to Geneva Auto Show 2020

The Rimac team has created 17 different prototypes which they're testing around the world to pull together a vehicle with the best performing components in it. The final prototype will be unveiled at the 2020 Geneva Auto Show. And, the 150 preordered vehicles will be delivered by late 2020

6. Electric Ford F-150 Pickup Truck

Source: Ford F-series Electric Truck Prototype

Assembled in Michigan for 2021

Ford is investing in electric vehicles in a very big way. In late 2019, it unveiled to rave review the Ford Mustang all-electric SUV, the Mach-E. And Ford has made good on a promise to electrify its highly popular F-150 pickup truck and to do so in its Michigan assembly plants with production likely in 2021.

UAW Contract

As part of its 4 year agreement with the UAW ratified in November 2019, Ford is pouring $6 billion into US plants for the production of electric and hybrid versions of the F-150 pickup along with autonomous vehicles and other products. Ford is also adding nearly 3,000 jobs to its Michigan workforce.

2021 Big Year

For Ford, the first autonomous vehicles will be completed in Michigan starting in 2021. The fully electric F-150 pickup will come shortly after that. This is part of Ford's $11.5 billion investment toward global electrified vehicles. Also in 2021, competitors like GM will deliver an electric truck and the Tesla Cybertruck will be coming out late that year. It's an accelerating electric vehicle future rolling into showrooms and onto highways near you.

7. Wisk Aero: Google's Larry Page & Boeing Flying EV

Source: Kitty Hawk's Cora

Big Push for Sustained Electric Powered Personal & Taxi Flight
Google founder Larry Page and his Kitty Hawk flying car startup are ramping up their alliance with aerospace giant Boeing to create electric flying vehicles. The vehicles are being categorized

as flying cars. But Page and Boeing are targeting VTOLs, vertical takeoff and landing vehicles that are fully electric powered and autonomous. The core R&D effort is Cora, an electric air taxi vehicle that was successfully tested in New Zealand. The Kitty Hawk-Boeing R&D partnership has been re-booted, re-branded and re-ignited as Wisk Aero and they are going full steam behind Cora.

VTOLs Are the Future of Personal Mobility
Kitty Hawk's Cora is a semiautonomous electric vehicle that seats two passengers. Their goal is to make Cora fully autonomous and electric. Kitty Hawk believes Cora will be ideal to fly people as an air taxi in congested urban areas. Boeing brings massive scale and aerospace expertise to the future of this important development project.

Self-Flying Vehicles verses Self-Driving Cars
Kitty Hawk in October 2019 unveiled a single person flying vehicle called Heaviside and predicted that self-flying vehicles will happen before self-driving cars. For investors the research & development being done on flying electric vehicles is noteworthy and something worth tracking.

8. VW's Electric Muscle Car: Prototype VW ID GTX

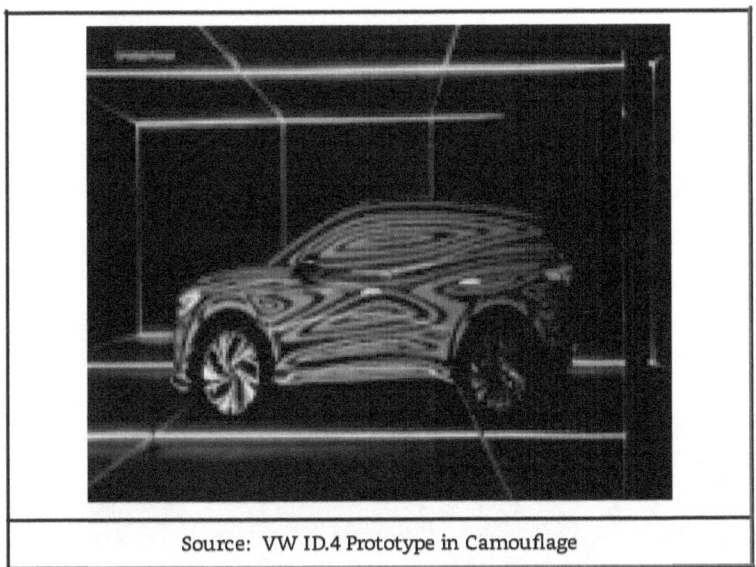
Source: VW ID.4 Prototype in Camouflage

GTX or Muscle Car

VW is planning on using the GTX moniker, meaning muscle car, for high performance versions of its all-electric lineup of vehicles rolling out in the 2020's. VW is keeping information tight on this and is even camouflaging images of the vehicle called the VW ID GTX.

Expectations of the VW ID GTX

The vehicle is expected to be very high performance, all-wheel drive, with dual electric motors which should give the vehicle extra power and firmer grip on the road. Reports indicate that a 2-door version of the ID.4 GTX could launch in Europe in 2021.

GTX Namesake

The GTX namesake goes back to 1967. It was on the Plymouth Belvedere GTX and lasted about two years. But among car lovers GTX is synonymous with muscle car. VW has already trade-marked GTX for the new, all-electric vehicle.

9. Cadillac Invests Big in EVs for 2020's

Source: Cadillac Escalade

Leading the E-Way for GM

Cadillac plans to be your electric vehicle brand of choice. And, the luxury brand is leading the electrification way for GM. Cadillac intends to have its total vehicle lineup with electrification versions by 2030. CEO Steve Carlisle does not know how long and how the repositioning from plants producing internal combustion engines to electric engines will take and how that will evolve. Understandably that's a work in progress as technology evolves. But, he does know the change to electric vehicles will happen. Carlisle projects that all or the majority of Cadillacs will be electrified by 2030. Ironically, Cadillac's 3Q 2019 global sales were up 8.8% much of which is from combustion engine car sales.

Escalade Evolving

Cadillac intends to power its full-sized SUV Escalade with an electric engine. In February 2020, a next-G Escalade will debut in Los Angeles with Super Cruise hands-free driving. More innovation is coming. Cadillac has been one of GM's leading brands in technology and innovation. Most of its customers love electric car innovation. Cadillac is GM's electric vehicle brand. It has an all-electric crossover coming to market in 2020 and more after that. It appears the Escalade will be leading the way.

10. Ultimate Electric Car: Ferrari Going Electric

Source: Ferrari SF90 Stradale Hybrid

Ferrari's Hybrid: Their Most Powerful Car

Ferrari is going all-electric. CEO Louis Camilleri told reporters he anticipates the all-electric Ferrari will come out sometime around 2025. It's coming in a few years because Camilleri says the battery technology isn't where it should be yet, including the need for faster recharging. He also wants advanced autonomous systems. Camilleri sees the advanced technology coming together to create Ferrari's first all-electric car by the mid-2020's.

Ferrari Now Focused on Hybridization

Ferrari's newest model, the SF90 Stradale, is the company's most powerful car ever. And, it's a plug-in hybrid. The vehicle packs 986 horsepower, reaches 60 mph in 2.5 seconds and has maximum speeds of 211 mph. Ferrari is focusing on hybridization now and hopes to have a 60% hybrid lineup by 2022, when it will introduce its first SUV. Meanwhile, the all-electric Ferrari is being developed on a GT (Grand Touring) platform for its introduction in the mid-2020's.

11. Hyundai's Massive R&D Investment in Electric, Autonomous & Flying Cars

Source: Hyundai Kona EV

Delivering Future of Mobility by 2025

Hyundai is pouring $52 billion into the development of electrics cars, self-driving cars, flying cars, robotics for them and an "ecosystem of mobility". The South Korean automaker says it wants to be a frontrunner in the future mobility industry. By 2025, Hyundai wants to trade in the name "automaker" for "smart mobility solutions provider".

Ecosystem of Mobility

Hyundai is the parent company of Kia and Hyundai. The $52 billion R&D investment will go into two strategic areas. One is more futuristic personal mobility vehicles like flying cars. The other is accelerating traditional autos forward with electrification, self-driving systems, robotics and "last mile mobility". By that Hyundai wants to combine products and services to deliver an "ecosystem of mobility" in the next decade.

Very Affordable EVs

Hyundai wants to sell 670,000 electric and fuel-cell vehicles yearly by 2025. It plans on delivering very affordable EVs to attract young buyers. And by 2025 it plans on delivering some level of self-driving performance in all of its vehicles. For investors, these big plans and big trends are something to follow.

12. Debut of VW Electric Hatchback in 2020

Source: Volkswagen Concept VW ID.3

One of 15 New EVs Set to Launch in 2020

A new wave of high style, long range and attractively priced electric vehicles will start rolling out in 2020 and throughout the new decade. Of the 15 new electric vehicles set to launch in 2020, a top contender is the VW ID.3 hatchback.

Electric Driving Future

The all-electric, VW ID.3 is a five door hatchback that will hit showrooms in early 2020. The vehicle is much anticipated and has been cited as one of the top five entrants into the electric vehicle driving market. VW has four electric vehicle concepts that it's been developing. Besides the VW ID.3, the ID.Vizzion, ID.Crzz and ID.Buzz are in the development pipeline. All of these vehicles will have a 250 mile range on one charge.

2019 EVs

In 2019 there werre about 50 EV models for sale in the US. The new decade will usher in 100 new EVs during the first few years. VW is a big part of the picture. The automaker says it will produce 22 million EV's by 2029. As VW puts it "We're plugged in".

VW Targets Greater Efficiencies
Meanwhile, VW's Production Chief Andreas Tostmann says VW's factories in Germany are set to boost efficiency to ramp up their competitiveness with other global automaking operations. He's targeting $2.2 billion in savings through greater efficiencies by 2023.

13. India Targets 2 Wheeler Bikes to be Electric by 2026

Source: New Delhi Street stock image

India's Government Sees EV Future
India is working on a plan to require that all 2-wheel vehicles, such as mopeds, motorbikes and scooters, be electric by 2026. That is a very big deal. 2-wheel vehicles are the dominant form

of transportation in India. Of the 250 million registered vehicles, 190 million are 2-wheel vehicles.

Global EV Capital

The government of Prime Minister Narenda Modi is strongly committed to an EV future. In fact, the government is accelerating incentives for the production of EV's and for consumer purchases of EV's. A number of new startups are springing up creating e-scooters, e-mopeds and e-bikes. India has a goal to become a global capital of EV manufacturing.

Cleaner, Greener Driving

For India much is at stake. It is a huge consumer of crude oil to power the 250 million vehicles, which in turn spew toxic emissions into the air. A recent study indicates that vehicle emissions in India caused 74,000 premature deaths and more than $20 billion in damage. The government's EV plan has been evolving but it is clearly committed to accelerating the use of electric vehicles. And it has the backing of the giant India conglomerate Tata Group, including Tata Power and Tata Motor, to build 300 rapid, recharging stations in five major cities by 2021.

14. **GM & LG's $2.3 Billion EV Battery Plant for Lordstown, Ohio**

Source: GM Electric Cadillac

GM and South Korea's LG Chem Joint Venture

GM and South Korea's LG Chem are investing $2.3 billion to build an electric vehicle battery cell plant in the Lordstown area of Ohio, USA. The plant will be one of the world's largest EV battery cell producing plants. GM and LG Chem will break ground for the new facility in mid-2020 and the new plant will create 1100 jobs at the start of operations. The companies say this plant will be flexible enough to respond to rapid changes in EV battery technology needs. Those needs are accelerating with demand for greater battery range on less charge times as electric car technology advances. Current electric batteries are very expensive.

GM CEO Mary Barra's Electric Vehicle Commitment

This is a very significant investment. GM CEO Mary Barra believes that the future of driving is electric. The lack of lithium-ion battery supplies, persistent production problems and the pressing need for new batteries that provide quicker charging with longer range are the major hurdles now constricting the rapid global expansion of the electric vehicle industry. Global demands for electric vehicles are dramatically growing in response to tightening regulations on gas and diesel fuel vehicle emissions to combat climate change.

Lordstown Plant
GM CEO Barra says the plant will be equally owned by LG Chem and GM for the mass production of battery cells for EVs. Importantly, the JV aims to drive down the costs of batteries for EV's and increase their profitability...all of which is designed to accelerate the future mass production and use of electric cars.

GM's Electric Future
The new Lordstown, Ohio plant will have the capacity of 30 gigawatt hours plus with room to expand. Also, GM says it's producing a new line of battery electric vehicles, including a new battery electric truck to be unveiled in the fall of 2021. For investors, these are significant developments paving the way to the EV future that merit watching.

15. Tesla Gets a Run for its Money

Source: Volvo Polestar 2 Electric Sedan

Big E-Competition from Volvo and BMW

The 2020's are expected to be the decade of electric vehicles. Every major automaker is planning to electrify its vehicle line-ups. For the first time, some global automakers will offer more electric and hybrid than conventional, gas and diesel powered vehicles. There are projections that by 2030 electric cars will amount to more than 20% of all new cars sold in the US.

Mass Market Electric Vehicles

Two electric cars expected to be important to a wide consumer audience are coming out during 2020 from BMW and Volvo. These cars are designed and priced to give Tesla a run for its electric vehicle money.

BMW i4

The 2020 BMW i4, a 4-door, fastback styled electric vehicle, is expected to hit the market in 2020 and be an important factor. Entry level models will be priced at less than $40,000. Reports indicate this vehicle can get 340 to 435 miles on a single charge, which offers Tesla significant competition. More details will come out on the BMW i4 from upcoming auto shows in 2020 during which BMW will provide more information.

Volvo's Polestar 2

Volvo also has a big ace up its sleeve in the all-electric Polestar 2 priced at $40,000. The compact, all-electric sedan packs 400 horsepower and a 311 mile range on a charge. The final product will roll out in 2020 and is expected to be a major player in the EV global market.

16. Porsche Forecasts Record 2020 US Sales Led by All Electric Taycan

Source: Porsche Electric-Taycan Sports Car

Electric Sports Car that's Eco Friendly with Speed

Porsche says its new, all-electric sports car Taycan is getting a lot of surprisingly big interest from Tesla electric car owners. This may be the first lap of the all-electric global car races for customer sales. According to VW-owned and German based Porsche, of the thousands of potential customers expressing interest in the Taycan, Tesla owners rank first among non-Porsche owners. Tesla is based in the US and founded and run by billionaire entrepreneur Elon Musk. The Taycan electric sports car is one of the most anticipated EVs of the upcoming decade for many technology reasons.

Electric Stats

The Taycan all-electric sports car delivers everything and all the power that you'd expect from a Porsche. It has 670 horsepower and goes from 0 to 60 mph in three seconds. Acceleration, speed by electric motors and zero free emissions. It has an estimated battery range of 300 miles, top speeds of 155 mph on a race track and the pricing starts at $103,800. The technology suite included in the sports car is awesome. It is a look at the electric future of driving with top of the line technology.

Electrifying Record Sales

Porsche in going with its first all-electric vehicle appears to be paying off in a big way. In 2020, Porsche is forecasting that the Taycan will catapult the company into record US retail sales. If so, that's a great example of a very expensive R&D investment by an automotive company to develop an all-electric sports car resulting in record US sales. The Taycan is looking like an electric car that's great for the environment and also great for the bottom line.

17. Electric Hybrid Aircraft from Airbus

Source: Airbus. E-Thrust Concept Electric Hybrid Aircraft

Cleaner, Greener Flying

Airbus is moving forward on plans to produce hybrid electric planes for commercial use by 2035. This is part of Airbus' major focus to develop and manufacture low emissions aircraft. Global air travel spews millions of tons of carbon dioxide from jet fuel into the atmosphere. Airbus CEO Guillaume Faury confirmed that he's moving ahead with the industry's first program to potentially develop and produce fleets of hybrid electric aircraft. He confirmed his electric hybrid plane goals during a conversation with reporters in late 2019.

E-Thrust Concept: Electric-Hybrid Flying Commitment with Greatly Reduced Emissions

Airbus' commitment to developing greener energy sources to power jets is clear. In May 2019, Airbus and SAS Scandinavian Airlines signed an agreement to partner on research for electric and hybrid aircraft designs. Their E-Thrust concept is an example of the future of flying with a serial hybrid propulsion system.

Airbus A320neo

Airbus is looking to replace its big seller, A320neo, narrow-body jets in the next 15 years. Airbus going with the industry's first electric hybrid aircraft would be a major technological breakthrough for the global airline industry. It would usher in the beginning of reducing utilization of jet fuel and cutting carbon dioxide emissions from the air.

Revolutionary Propulsion System

The European plane maker is growing in confidence about its revolutionary propulsion system with hybrid electric engines ready to power a new single aisle jet by 2035. The company is expected to start with a smaller electric hybrid jet and work up to a full size jet that would be capable of carrying 240 people. It's the future of electric flying that investors should keep track of.

18. BMW & Tesla Expanding Production of EVs in China

Source: BMW MINI Cooper

BMW Grows China Presence

BMW is significantly expanding its global electric vehicle operations. BMW and its Chinese partner Great Wall announced that they plan to build a $716 million plant in China big enough to manufacture 160,000 electric cars a year. The plant will produce electric MINI's for BMW and also Great Wall electric vehicles. Great Wall is China's #1 SUV and pickup truck manufacturer. Meanwhile, US-based Tesla set a new record with its electric pick-up Cybertruck.

Big China Electric Vehicle Market Expansions
The BMW-Great Wall plant is due to open in 2022 near Shanghai. For e-car makers, the opportunity in China is huge. China has new quotas starting in 2025 requiring that 20% of total vehicle sales are electric and rechargeable hybrids. Automakers and suppliers are diligently working to meet these tough, new, antipollution standards that China is enforcing. VW is opening two plants in China with a combined production capacity of 600,000 electric vehicles per year. And, Tesla has opened a new plant in Shanghai to produce 500,000 electric vehicles per year.

Tesla's Cybertruck
In December 2019, Tesla founder and CEO Elon Musk's electric Cybertruck orders hit a new record. 250,000 customers signed up to buy the muscle, e-pickup truck within one week of launch, despite the shattered "bulletproof" windows that broke twice when hit by metallic balls during the big debut. Production of Cybertruck is targeted for 2022 so engineer Musk has time to fix the glass

19. Lincoln's 2022 Electric SUV

Source: Rivian. Top - e-platform. Bottom - Rivian R1S SUV

Startup Rivian Forging the Way with Unique E-Vehicle Platform

Reports indicate that Lincoln will be a big beneficiary of Ford's $500 million investment in Detroit e-vehicle startup Rivian. Amazon is also investing in the company. Lincoln is expected to use Rivian's skateboard-styled platform for a Lincoln electric SUV coming out in 2022. This would be the first example of Ford's plans to co-develop a vehicle based on Rivian's electric car platform.

Rivian's e-Vehicles

Rivian's platform is a highly modular, battery-electric design. It resembles a skateboard. The system can deliver up to 700 horsepower. It fits batteries up to 180 kilowatt hours in size. Rivian is using the platform for its own R1T pick-up truck and R1S SUV that will go into production in late 2020. Rivian says the SUV gets 400 miles in range on a charge. And in 30 minutes, the batteries charge to add an additional 200 miles in range.

Ford Going Electric

Ford is significantly investing in electric vehicles. In fact, it is separately developing its own electric vehicle platform. One is on the Ford 2021 Mustang Mach-E, the all-electric SUV, based on the iconic Mustang brand.

20. Tesla, GM, Ford E-Charging Ahead

Source: Tesla

Big SUV and Pickup Truck Green Driving
Tesla's all-electric Cybertruck picked up 250,000 orders in the week following its December 2019 launch in Los Angeles. That's a big deal. People love the sleek armored truck look and power of the electric muscle truck that is Tesla CEO Elon Musk's pet project. Engineer Musk made the truck of the same steel he uses at Space X for his rockets. Buyers apparently forgave the faux paus of the bullet proof windows shattering twice when hit by a metallic ball at its debut. Production on Cybertruck starts in two years. Prices start at $40,000 and the vehicle has a battery range on the top class model of 500 miles. Musk has some time to work on the shattered glass of the shatterproof windows.

All Electric Pickup Wars
GM announced it will deliver an all-electric pickup truck by fall of 2021. Ford will deliver on an all-electric pickup truck F150 at

about the same time. And a Detroit based startup Rivian, which is backed by Amazon and Ford, will start producing its own electric pickup in 2020. The e-pickup category is very hot and congested with competition. The reason is that pickups are hot, accounting for 17% of US light vehicle volume sales and a staggering 70% of the profits.

All Electric Crossovers

Meanwhile, electric crossover vehicles are a super charged market. Ford just unveiled its 2021 Mustang Mach-E all electric SUV to rave reviews as a revival of the iconic sports brand. The Mach-E will take on Tesla Model Y, a compact e-SUV that goes into production in 2020. BMW, Audi and Mercedes are also all in the game. In all, 100 electric vehicles will be hitting global showrooms in the next couple of years.

.

21. Ford's Latest Mustang is an Electric SUV

Fully Electric, Mustang SUV

In late 2019, Ford unveiled its long awaited, brand new Ford Mustang. Mach-E, the Mustang inspired vehicle, is a fully electric SUV. Ford is taking reservations - a $500 deposit is required - but, you'll have to wait awhile for delivery. Ford says production will start on the Mach-E at a Ford facility in Mexico in the 4th quarter of 2020.

Sleek, Green Vehicle with Performance

The Mach-E is a 5-passenger crossover electric SUV with style and performance inspired by the original Mustang. The Mustang is an iconic vehicle, treasured by many, that dates back to the 1960's. The latest iteration on the Mustang theme was unveiled by Ford Executive Chairman Bill Ford and actor Idris Elba in Los Angeles (photo above) in late November 2019.

Important Details

The Mach-E is priced to start at $50,000 which experts say may give Tesla a run for its money. The vehicle has a range of up to 300 miles. Ford expects this electric SUV to be profitable from day one. The top of the line, high performance GT model has all-wheel drive and does a zero-to-60 in 3 seconds.

SECTION TWO: ROBOTIC INNOVATIONS

22. Ebo CatPal: Robotic Companion for Your Cat

Real-Time Monitor and Playmate for Home Alone Cats

It's called the Ebo CatPal. The device is designed to keep your pet cat happy, occupied and prevent boredom by providing the cat with fun interaction and exercise with a smart, robotic companion. This robot is loaded with advanced technology:

- CatPal has AI algorithms to detect the cat's mood and adapt to the cat's style of play
- It connects to WiFi to enable the owners to monitor the cat with sound and video, providing access anywhere
- There's a 1080pHD camera to live stream the cat
- Ebo's movements are autonomous and it can wheel, roll and dance on its own with the assistance of collision sensors
- Ebo's eyes, sounds and movements mimic real-life play

- It self-returns to its charging block to recharge when needed

Cat-Proof

Ebo is ruggedly cat-proof and round. After scanning a room for obstacles, it rolls about on its own power, makes noises and flashes its LED eyes. 60% of US cats are overweight so the exercise Ebo provides for the cat is a key benefit. The little robot has an embedded microphone and camera. It can also be manually controlled by the owners with a paired device. The device is available on Kickstarter with a price of $159.00

23. New, Fast Acting Soft Robots Expandable & High Speeds

Bioinspired by Chameleons, Salamanders and Toads

Researchers at Purdue University have invented a new class of high speed, soft robots and actuators. They are bio-inspired by the high speed, elastic motions of salamanders, chameleons and toads that launch their tongues in a tenth of a second to catch an insect. Purdue's new soft robot can catch a live, flying beetle in the same way, in a blink of an eye. This robotic innovation is big for potential use in accelerated automation.

New Class of Soft Robots

The Purdue scientists' new innovation is a new class of entirely soft robots and actuators. They are capable of recreating bioinspired high powered, high speed motion using stored elastic energy. They're composed of stretchable polymers like a rubber band with channels that expand with pressurization.

Amazing Robotics

This robot expands five times in length and can catch a live flying beetle in 120 milliseconds. The robot's elastic energy is stored by stretching its body during fabrication. The scientists believe such high speed robotics could achieve automated tasks more accurately and much faster. This is robotic innovation to be watched by investors for commercialization.

24. **Microrobots with Controlled Flight: Harvard's RoboBees**

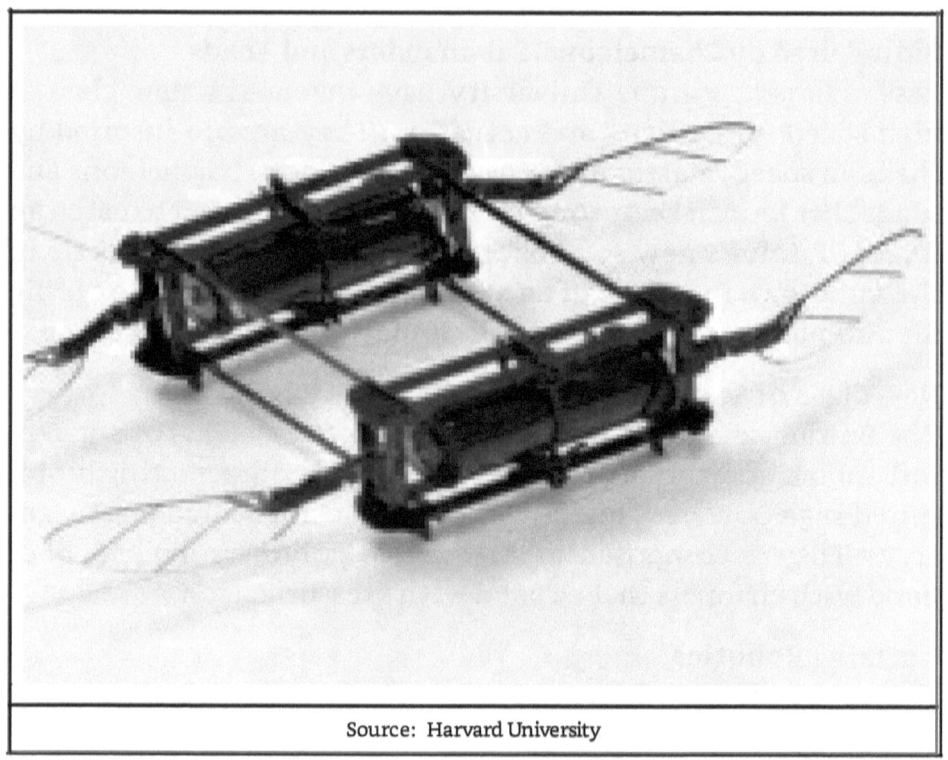

Source: Harvard University

Search & Rescue Missions

Harvard's RoboBees are the first microbots powered by soft actuators to achieve controlled flight. They have soft artificial muscles that enable them to survive crashes and collisions making them perfect for search and rescue missions in dangerous, cluttered environments. The robobees are so sturdy, dexterous and resilient they can even crash into a wall or collide with another robobee without any damage.

Hoverbots

The tiny robots are equipped with actuators made from dielectric elastomers that deform when hit with an electrical current. The actuators are soft and the Harvard team says they're easily assembled and scaled up. Unlike other drones made with soft actuators, the robobees have enough power density to hover in place.

Going for Commercialization

The Harvard team has created a number of models including one with 8 wings and 4 actuators that can do controlled hovering flight, which is a first. They feel the sky is the limit for the number of robots of this type that they can build. Harvard's Office of Technology Development has protected the intellectual property of this invention and is exploring commercialization. This is important new technology that investors will want to watch developments, particularly on commercialization.

25. New Robotic Innovation from Technical University of Munich

Source: Technical University of Munich

Touch Sensitive Artificial Skin Makes for Safer, Accident Avoid-

ing Robots

This is new innovation from the Technical University of Munich. Their H-1 autonomous, humanoid robot is covered with touch sensitive, synthetic artificial skin. The skin is composed of 13,000 separate sensors. The sensors enable the robot to feel the touch of humans. New algorithms made it possible to apply artificial skin to a human sized robot.

Safer Working Robots

This is an important development because of concerns about humans getting hurt working side by side with robots. Biologically-inspired artificial skin improves the robot's sensory ability, making it possible for the robot to sense its own body and surroundings.

Senses Like the Human Brain

The robot's artificial skin is able to measure temperature, pressure, proximity and acceleration. The sensors are an event-based system that transmits information only when a value is changed. It works in a manner similar to the human nervous system and reduces the computer processing demand by 90%. The artificial skin helps the robot to operate safer when near people and gives it the ability to anticipate and actively avoid accidents.

26. Drones with Unlimited Fly Times: Inflight Battery Swaps

Source: UC Berkeley New Drone/Battery System

UC Berkeley HiPeRLab Innovation

Can you imagine a drone with almost unlimited flying time? Well, it's been created by engineers and roboticists at the University of California Berkeley's HiPeRLab, their High Performance Robotics Lab. It's a prototype drone system with unique, inflight battery switching technology. The potential is to keep drones in the air for almost unlimited flight times.

Quadcopter Drone with a Docking Deck

The team has invented a quadcopter drone with a docking tray that's able to accept a smaller, fresh battery delivering drone. The battery drone lands on the dock, recharges the larger drone and flies away. This allows the next battery drone to fly in and take its place to do a recharge.

Sustainable Drone Flights

This is a fascinating approach to one way of powering sustainable drone flights. In the future, others might include solar or wind power combinations. The UC High Performance Robotics Lab advances Unmanned Aerial Systems' capabilities by advanced algorithms, mechanical design and control strategies. You might call it hyper performance robotics.

27. Shapeshifter Drone Exploring New Distant Worlds

Source: NASA

Drone of Drones

NASA's Jet Propulsion Lab at Caltech has introduced the drone of drones. It separates into two different units: two shapes to explore new distant worlds and new habitats. It's a prototype and is made of several small, quadcopter drones calls cobots. The cobots have propellers and fly independently and the system reassembles to roll on the ground. The future for the concept is much bigger. The Shapeshifter would be made up of a number of small robots that can easily self-assemble into larger robots and disassemble as the mission requires, particularly in space. The mini-robots will be able to fly, roll, float and swim and then morph into a single machine.

Morphing Robots

On the ground, the cobots come together to form a roller-wheel like drone to explore the ground in places in space like Titan, where there is very limited information about the surface. The unpredictability of the surface makes versatility and shapeshifting essential in the drone. In the future, the plan is to make the cobots work together as a team of twelve to explore caves, underwater areas and various types of terrain, including in outer space. The ultimate morphing robot team would be carried aboard a mothership lander that would house their energy source and scientific instrumentation for testing and analysis.

Dragonfly 2026

This extraordinary technology will take quite a few years to fully develop. But a target for it is 2026 when NASA's Dragonfly drone takes off for Titan with possibly the Shapeshifter onboard. The Shapeshifter is a transformational vehicle to explore, treacherous, distant and not-so-distant worlds.

28. Tunabot - Fast as Tuna, Next G Underwater Vehicle Propulsion

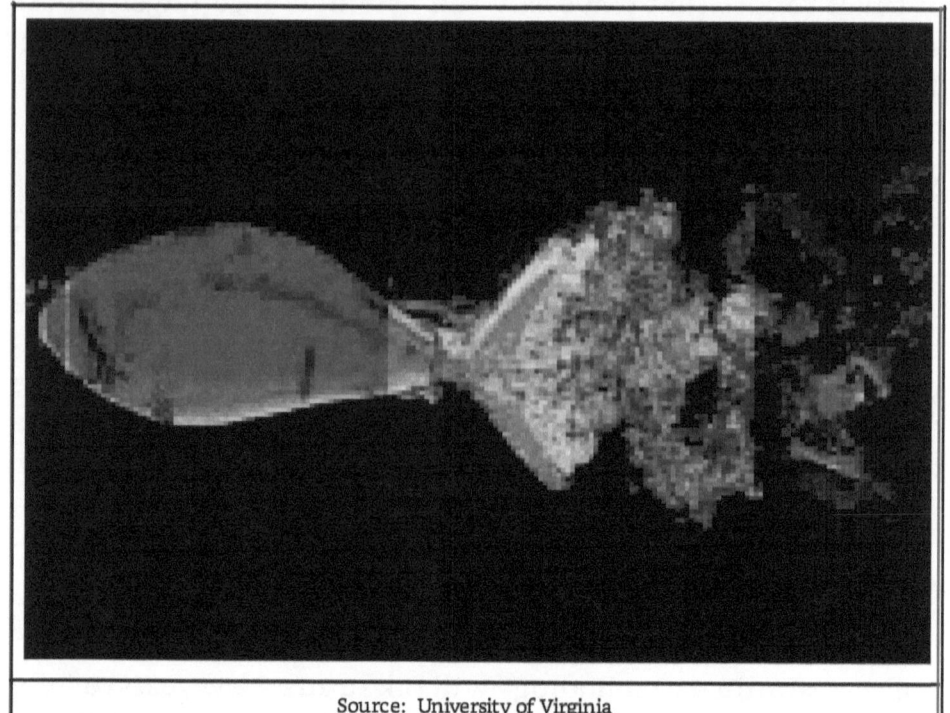

Source: University of Virginia

Prototype for Next G Underwater Vehicle Propulsion

The tuna is one of the fastest fish in the sea. A mechanical engineering team from University of Virginia in collaboration with biologists from Harvard University have invented a robofish that can swim as fast as a yellowfin tuna. The team says it's not about the robot. It's about inventing a new, faster and more efficient underwater propulsion system for manned and unmanned underwater vehicles.

Physics of Fish Propulsion

At Harvard and UVA, Tunabot is tethered in a large flow tank with a green laser to measure fluid motion as it swims. Yellowfin tuna grow to 7 feet. The Tunabot is 10 inches long. The purpose of this research is to better understand the physics of fish propulsion to develop the next generation of underwater vehicles with fish like propulsion system. The team says the ultimate goal "is to surpass biology" with new, quicker and more efficient propulsion.

According to the researchers, Tunabot is the world's fastest robot fish right now in 2020.

Surpassing Biology

The device has been tested at both Harvard and UVA. It can swim with a maximum speed equal to the real fish, which is 4 body lengths per second. Tunabot's body is flexible and it swims just like a tuna. With a 10 watt battery pack, it can go 1.3 feet per second for a distance of 5.6 miles. If the speed is increased to 3.3 feet per second, the range is 2.5 miles. This is just the beginning for this new technology. It could possibly be used for underwater surveillance, as part of the funding is from the US Office of Naval Research. But the aim is beyond that: a brand new, innovative propulsion system for underwater vehicles that is bio-inspired.

29. MIT's Roboats that Change Shape & Form Bridges

Source: MIT

Autonomous Boats that Disconnect and Reassemble
This is the world's first bridge composed of autonomous boats that disconnect and reassemble into various configurations. It's the invention of engineers and other scientists at MIT and the Amsterdam Institute for Advanced Metropolitan Solutions. The city of Amsterdam has big plans for them in their canals to reduce busy traffic on congested city streets.

Amsterdam Deployment
Amsterdam wants the roboats to cruise its 165 canals to transport people and goods, collect trash and self-assemble into pop-up platforms like bridges and stages as needed. The roboats are equipped with sensors, thrusters, GPS modules, cameras, microcontrollers and other hardware. They are far less expensive and far more versatile than traditional bridges.

New Algorithm Upgrade
The roboats have been upgraded with a new control algorithm that enables them to be "shapeshifting", autonomously changing into floating platforms, floating stages, floating crossways and bridges. They can also adapt from transporting people to opening up in order to allow boats to pass through. The roboats autonomously travel in the water and dock and lock with each other, depending on what operational mode is needed.

New Form of Transportation
MIT Professor Carlo Ratti, who is the lead developer, says the system can connect two sides of a canal by using autonomous boats "that become dynamic, responsive architecture that float on water."

30. Astro May Be One of the World's Smartest Dogs

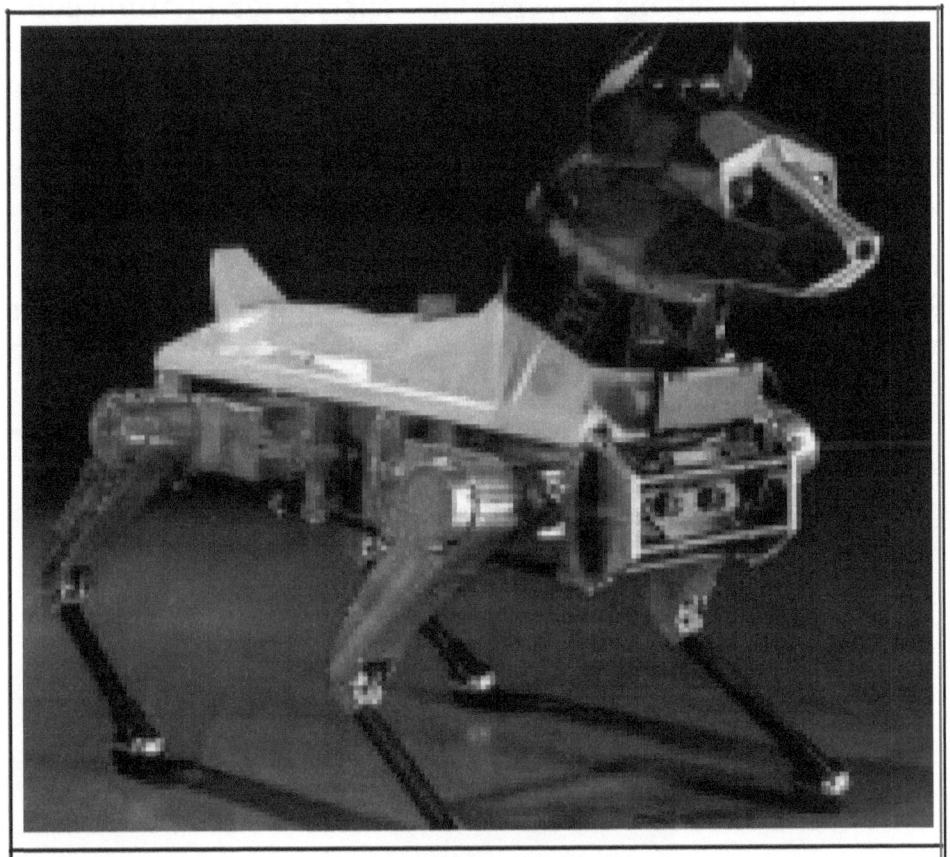

Source: Florida Atlantic University

New Invention from Florida Atlantic University Roboticists

Astro is a deep learning and artificial intelligence powered, quadruped robodog created by a team of roboticists and other experts at Florida Atlantic University. Like your dog, it learns by trial and error. It has a deep neural network that enables it to learn and perform tricks. Astro's 3D printed head is designed to resemble a Doberman and has a computerized brain. The team calls it "a puppy in training" but already it can sit, stand and lie down. The robot can see and hear.

Loaded with Technology

Astro contains cameras, high tech radar sensors, radar imaging and a directional microphone. Most importantly, it has four teraflops of processing power or the capacity for 4 trillion computations per second with its Nvidia Jetson TX2 graphics processing units. All of this technology allows it to be trained like a dog. The FAU team says Astro will be able to respond to hand signals, identify colors, understand different languages, coordinate with drones, recognize faces and a lot more.

Future for Astro
Right now, Astro is a "puppy" learning new commands but this is not just fun and games. For Astro, future functions include bomb detection, search and rescue, work as a service dog, medical diagnosis monitoring and potentially even making real-time decisions based on experience.

SECTION THREE: SUSTAINABLE PRODUCT INNOVATIONS

31. Latest Brilliant Idea from Tesla's Elon Musk

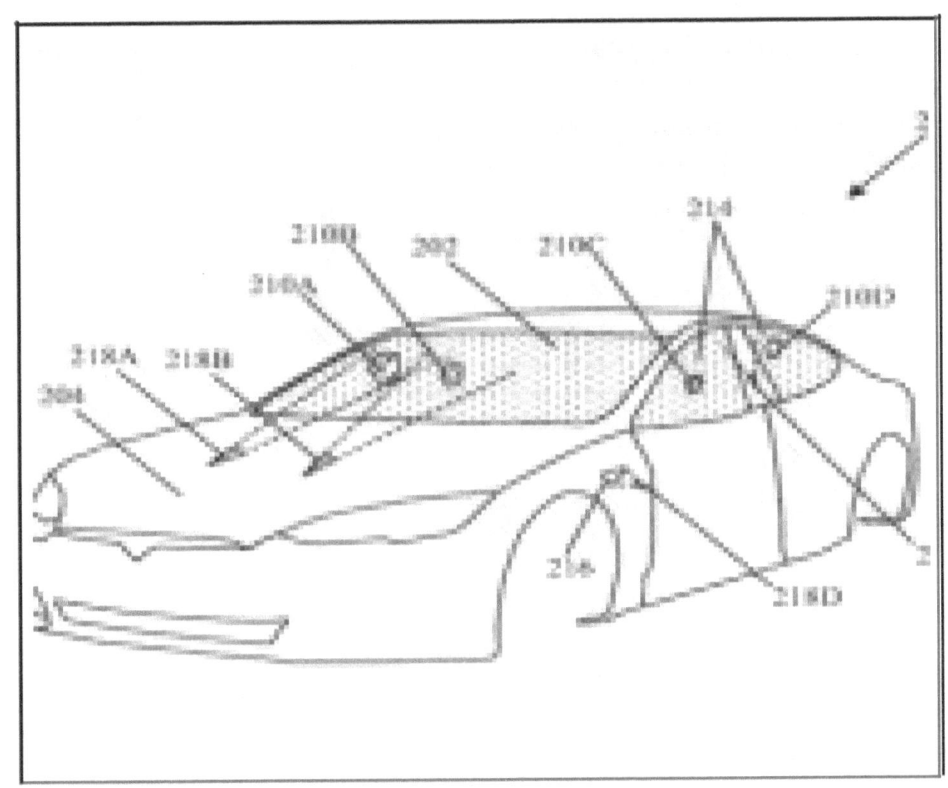

Source: Tesla Patent Filing

Virtual Light Show Around Your Car

Tesla founder and CEO Elon Musk has filed for a patent on his latest idea: replacing car windshield wipers with laser beams. The billionaire engineer, who also founded and is the CEO of SpaceX, has big plans for this laser innovation. His first goal is to replace windshield wipers with laser beam wipers.

Light Technology

The system uses pulsed lasers and detection circuitry to identify debris on the windshield and direct a laser to remove it. It calibrates the amount of laser light needed to do the job. According to the patent application the system is sensitive and smart enough to differentiate wanted items like a car inspection sticker and not remove it.

Additional Uses

In addition to keeping car windshields clean and clear, the system can be deployed to remove dirt from cameras that direct autonomous cars. It can also clean solar panels on the car to keep the panels more efficient. Entrepreneur Elon Musk is developing an autonomous, electric light show on wheels.

32. Sustainable Bobsla Bobsled Invented in Austria

Source: Bobsla

Riding Through the Alps

It's called the Bobsla and it's a unique electric vehicle invention. Bobsla is an electric bobsled vehicle that's similar to a go-cart on the snow. The Innsbruck-based startup Bobsla GmbH has successfully tested the device and it's taking riders for exhilarating rides through the Alps. The inventors say it's easy to learn, safe and is designed as an alternative to snowmobiling and skiing.

Electricity on Ice
The device has a rear-mounted electric motor that can accelerate up to 18 mph. It's quiet and more affordable than a snowmobile. The inventors say it's great for snowy tourist destination. It offers non-skiers something more exciting to do by taking rides in the snow.

Mercedes Challenge
According to the Bobsla's website, the company and the device have been invited by Mercedes to participate in the Sprinter Startup challenge. The inventors consider their Bobsla part snowmobile and part draft kart. It certainly is unique new technology to enjoy the snow in a green, electric vehicle without sending toxic emissions into the atmosphere.

33. Sustainable Listening: Solar Powered Headphones

Source: JBL

Totally Green Sound from Light

The Reflect Eternal headphones from JBL generate power to operate from the natural light of the Sun and from artificial light. The self-charging headphones contain solar-charging material, Powerfoyle from Exeger, that is built into the headband. The material transforms light into free, sustainable energy. The headphones need only two hours of sun per day to provide 168 hours of listening. The headphones can be used indoors and outside and can recharge on artificial light.

Crowdfunding for Consumer Input

JBL is developing the Reflect Eternal headphones by collaborating directly with consumers by engaging them in crowdfunding on Indiegogo . They want to determine the level of consumer interest in such a green, sustainable product and then fine-tune the product from input. JBL is a long established audio company with products like ProSound. The JBL Reflect Eternal headphones are totally wireless and powered by next generation, green, solar power.

34. New Invention: Tablet Toothpaste, Tubeless Toothpaste

Source: Change Toothpaste

Potentially Cuts 900 Million Plastic Toothpaste Tube Throwaways Per Year

Tubes of toothpaste aren't something you think about but their impact on the global environment is hugely negative. 900 million toothpaste tubes are discarded into oceans and landfills globally every year. Importantly, it takes 500 years for them to breakdown, which means virtually every toothpaste tube created is still discarded someplace in the world. And, the tubes, which contain multiple layers of plastic, polymers and resins, can't be recycled. A company headquartered in Edmonton, Alberta Canada has come up with a solution in the form of tablet toothpaste.

"Paste with No Waste"
Entrepreneurs Mike Medicoff and Damien Vince are the inventors and founders of CHANGE Toothpaste. Their tablet toothpaste is an all-natural vegan substance that works just like toothpaste but has no harsh chemicals. You pop the pill in your mouth, crunch on it and scrub your teeth with a wet brush. They dub the product "Paste with No Waste", specifically no empty plastic tubs left behind.

Sustainability Mission and Crowdfunding Expansion
CHANGE Toothpaste's mission is to "enable sustainable consumption of everyday products, like toothpaste, by everyday people". The company was established in January 2019 and is now in the process of crowdfunding expansion. The tablets can be ordered and are packaged in 100% compostable paper pouches. Monthly orders of 65 tablets at $9.95 are available. The company says their product is a small change that reduces the consumer's environmental footprint. And if the toothpaste tablet trend takes hold, it could have a significant positive impact on the global environment.

35. Heatbox, the Self-Heating Lunchbox from the Netherlands

Source: Heatbox

Mobile Hot Meals

This is another example of great innovation from the Netherlands. Heatbox warms food with steam. The steam is created by the lunchbox's heating element working with a small amount of water. It was created by the Netherlands start-up Heatbox. The device is portable and small enough to fit in a backpack. It's rechargeable and can work multiple times a day. The smart lunchbox heats your food in minutes. It enables the user to have a hot meal wherever they are.

Heatbox and Your Phone

Heatbox can be controlled manually or by a smartphone app. It can even charge your cellphone. The device has a modern, sleek design. It appears to have great potential for students and anyone on the go. It's in the Kickstarter phase with product deliveries set for July 2020. It's a breakthrough gadget that provides mobile hot meals.

36. New Emergency Device Hand Cranked to Generate Power for Key Gadgets

Light Saber: Innovative Outdoor Survival Tool

The Light Saber outdoor survival technology tool was invented by the Innovation Factory, a US based company that's been making tough tools since 2001. Their Light Saber delivers limitless power supply to essential gadgets like cell phones by hand cranking it. It's limited only by your muscle power. It's a portable device that can deliver enough power to charge a cell phone with three minutes worth of hand cranking. It's designed to help adventurers survive in the outdoors and wilderness areas. It has an onboard battery that you can charge for the road.

Lots of Emergency Tech Included

This emergency device has a lot of new tech loaded in. It has a USB generator, emergency strobe lights and sirens, a UV water purifier and a plasma fire starter. The company calls it an inexhaustible power supply for wilderness survival.

37. Smart Suitcase Charges Devices by Spinning its Wheels

Source: ROLLOGO

Charging Your Gadgets on the Go

ROLLOGO is the world's first self-charging luggage that has wheels with a suspension system. It's a remarkable combination of engineering, style and design. Designed by well-known innovator/designer Frederic Gooris of Brussels, it's a very smart gadget to keep your smart gadgets charged when you're on the go. Importantly, this charging suitcase is TSA approved, according to ROLLOGO, so there's no problem at airport check-ins.

Spinning its Wheels

The ROLLOGO Escape S suitcase charges its power bank by spinning its wheels. The company calls it a new way to travel smarter and more sophisticated. Ten minutes of rolling wheels can create enough power to talk on your smartphone for an hour. The suitcase contains an 8000 mAh lithium polymer power bank, that's

65

recharged by the company's patented power generating wheel system. The fully charged power bank offers ten hours of charging.

Pairs with Apps

The smart, carry-on suitcase pairs with an app to show what battery time is left both on the suitcase and on your device. It also has an app to let you track the carry-on and provides alerts if it gets out of range. There's also an anti-theft device. ROLLOGO is designed to be a first class suitcase and there are other special features built into it. The device has surpassed its Kickstarter goals and should start shipping in April 2020. Interesting new travel tech!

38. Artificial, Magnetic Skin: New Wearable

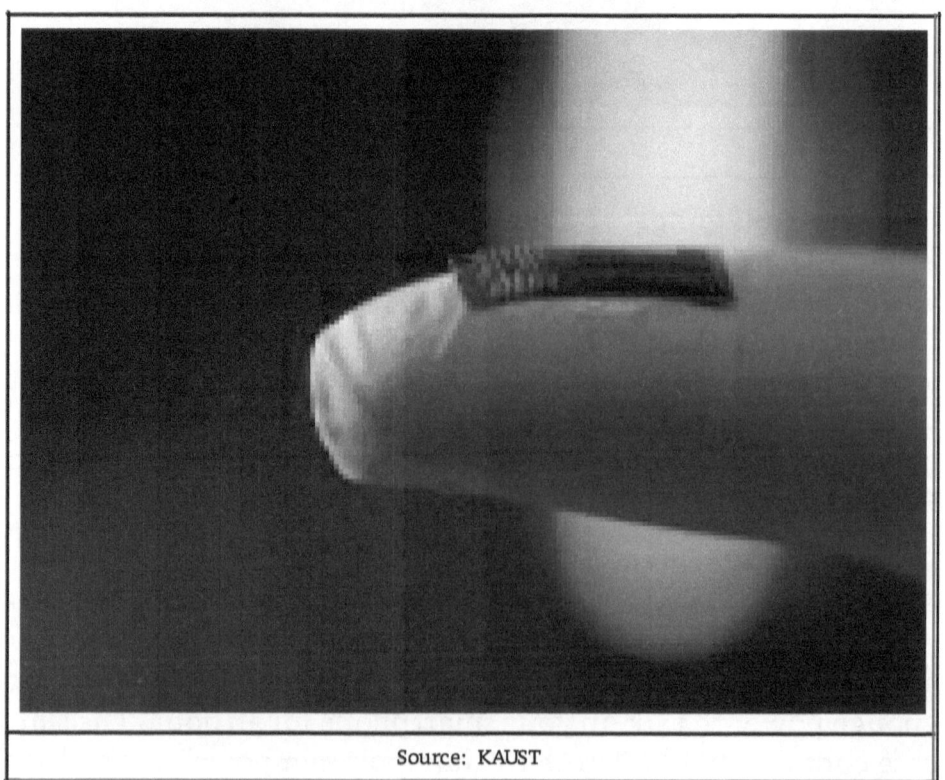

Source: KAUST

Breakthrough Innovation from Saudi Arabia

A team at KAUST, the King Abdullah University of Science and Technology, has developed a new, magnetic skin that could enable new, wearable consumer technology and assistive devices for the elderly and disabled. The skin is imperceptible, biocompatible and very innovative. The new tech ushers in a new generation of touch sensors with low-cost technology applications.

No Batteries or Wires Needed

What is remarkable is the skin doesn't require embedded electronics....no wires, batteries or antennas. The material is ultra flexible. It's powered by an elastomer matrix mixed with magnetic powder.

Tailor-Magnetized for Specific Uses

The skin is tailor-magnetized for specific applications. The uses include tracking eye movements to detect disease and robotic arms and prosthetics with haptic perception. The key innovator is KAUST PhD. candidate Ahmed Alfadhel who started by investigating nature's solutions for a sense of touch in animals like fish and crickets. He says these creatures have incredible mechanosensorial skin that allows them to feel "the imperceptible like the landing of a butterfly."

39. Smart Backpack Designed to Make Cyclists More Visible and Safer

Source: Roadwarez

Roadwarez Street Warrior Backpack

This is new safety innovation for cyclists. It's an intelligent, wearable backpack with a LED array that lights up and provides big, illuminated signals to the drivers, cyclists and people around you that you're turning or breaking. It's called the Roadwarez Street Warrior backpack. The company says it's the world's first automated cycling signaling system with an LED cycling back-pack and new app.

New Connected Tech

This system is designed to increase bikers' visibility and safety. Roadwarez says it's focused on the innovative integration of tech-nology and apparel. Street Warrior is enabled by Bluetooth. It also has accident detection technology and signals an alert if you are hit, providing your chosen contacts your location. The LED array can work manually or be pre-programmed by mapping your ride in the companion app. It also flashes in motion riding lights for added visibility. There's also microphone integration to speak commands to the system as you ride. And finally, this invention functions as a regular backpack with plenty of storage inside.

40. IBM's Seaweed Battery: Good For Environment

Source: IBM

IBM and Mercedes Partner to Commercialize

IBM has created a revolutionary battery that replaces the heavy metals in the cathode with 3 elements extracted from seawater. They are also utilizing a new type of liquid electrolyte. It's a safer, more "ethically sourced" and highly efficient new type of battery. The standard heavy metals used like nickel and cobalt are very harmful to the environment and pose humanitarian risks in mining. IBM says this new seawater battery outperforms lithium-ion batteries in major respects.

Already Going Commercial

This battery invention has the potential to be a blockbuster and is worthy of being tracked by investors. IBM says the battery can be optimized to surpass the capability of lithium-ion batteries in terms of lower costs, faster charging time, higher power and energy density, stronger energy efficiency and lower flammability. The big application is for electric vehicles. Mercedes-Benz is partnering with IBM to commercialize the new technology.

Long-Term Sustainability

IBM says their new battery invention could transform the long term sustainability of many parts of our energy infrastructure. The company is keeping details on the makeup of the battery under wraps. But we do know the battery rapidly charges at a pace of 80% in five minutes. And using elements from seawater as a key component make it sustainable and much better for the environment.

SECTION FOUR: CONNECTIVITY INNOVATIONS

41. World 1st Virtual Reality/Augmented Reality Windshield

Source: Futurus

Future of Driving: Augmented Reality, Electric, Autonomous, Smart Vehicles

The future of driving is zooming towards us and it is electric, autonomous and loaded with augmented reality. The Chinese technology company Futurus, based in Beijing, has new technology to convert the entire car front windshield of your car into a virtual reality screen. The transparent display is designed as a smart &/or autonomous human-machine interface platform. The Chinese scientists and engineers who invented it say it makes driving safer.

Cutting Edge Technology

This technology is a light screen projection system that provides a 60 degree field of view. The functionality seems impressive. It can alert drivers to hazards, display navigation guidance, play music, provide internet messages and social media. The windshield can even display entertainment for passengers. The entertainment isn't visible to the driver who can focus on the augmented reality of the road and surroundings before them.

Artificial Intelligence Enabled

This system is powered by artificial intelligence. The developers say it's meant to be integrated with driving assistance systems, information "push" systems, office and entertainment systems. It's a new look at the future of electric, autonomous, connected, smart driving with the added element of augmented and virtual reality displayed on the windshield to enhance safety.

42. Ford's Advanced New Connectivity for Cars

Source: Ford Electric Mustang SUV

Next G Vehicle Connectivity

Ford is rolling out huge internet connectivity for its vehicles. And, Ford is starting with the upcoming Ford Mustang Mach-E all-electric SUV. The electric Mustang will be leading edge for a new, highly advanced generation of internet connectivity that Ford will deploy in its future vehicle lineups.

Real-Time Monitoring of Vehicle Performance

Ford executives say this technology will take Ford's business to the next level. It will enable over-the-air software updates that will not require a trip to the dealership. New connectivity services for consumers will be available in the vehicles. And, the technology will allow Ford to closely monitor vehicle performance in real time, in the real world. Experts say the monitoring could go down to the level of individual parts in the car.

2021
Ford is taking $500 deposits and reservations for the Mach-E for delivery in 2021. Production of the iconic Mustang e-SUV starts in late 2020.

43. In China Facial Recognition Reaches Mobile Phones

Source: Facial ID Scanning Stock Image

May Prevent Fraud in Cyberspace But Does it Increase Citizen Surveillance?

This is a new use of facial recognition technology that the world is watching. China has regulations that require Chinese telecom operators to scan the faces of people registering for new mobile phone services in China. The consumer or business could be buying a new SIM card or any new mobile phone services. The purchaser has no choice but to have their face scanned. The Chinese government says it's combating cyber-fraud and protecting its citizens from being hacked. This is facial recognition at the cutting edge of use, controversy and possibly usefulness. Once your face is scanned on your mobile phone, anyplace you use it, such as in your home and stores, could be tracked.

Controversial

This could be viewed as a legitimate and ongoing push by China to ensure people are using the internet under their real names in order to prevent fraud and increase cybersecurity. Or it could be viewed as increased surveillance on Chinese citizens. Or the goals and objectives could include all of the above.

UN and World Are Watching

The Chinese deployment of facial recognition technology is being closely watched globally. There are no global standards for such ID tech yet. Potential global standards on the use of facial ID tech are being reviewed and will be set as standards by the United Nations. Interestingly, Chinese technology firms are participating in the UN effort. Stay tuned for this piece of innovative, disruptive technology in the middle of infringing on personal freedoms and protecting you from cyber-theft, right now playing in on a world stage in China.

44. World's 1st Camera System to Spot Drivers Handling Mobile Phones

Source: Sydney Highways Stock Image

New South Wales Using Tech to Cut Road Fatalities

Australia's state of New South Wales, where Sydney is located, has rolled out new technology along the roads to cut fatalities caused by distracted drivers on mobile phones. They're deploying high definition, AI-enabled detection cameras to spot drivers handling their mobile phones, which is illegal in New South Wales (NSW). 45 portable cameras, including fixed and mobile trailer mounted cameras, are being set-up in undisclosed locations. Authorities believe that within two year the surveillance system will cut the number of fatalities on its roads by one-third. This HD, AI camera system tech and application are a world first.

24-7 Roadside Detection

The high tech cameras work day, night and in all types of weather to detect if a driver going by is handling a mobile phone. The cameras use artificial intelligence to analyze images in order to spot drivers breaking the law. In NSW, it's legal to make and receive mobile calls on a hands-free mobile phone. It's illegal to manually use a mobile phone while driving. It's also illegal to be on social media with your mobile phone while driving. What the cameras spot is reviewed for verification by authorities.

Changing the Mobile Culture

In NSW in 2019, 329 people lost their lives in driving fatalities on the roads. With the new camera detection devices, authorities expect to nab 135 million vehicles with drivers breaking the mobile phone laws every year. They believe that will cut road fatalities 30% by 2021. Authorities call it a system to change the mobile phone culture. After a first warning, offenders will get a stiff fine, penalty points and escalating consequences with repeated offenses.

45. Grocery Shopping with No Checkout Lines

Source: Amazon

Amazon Tech - Amazon Go

Amazon is introducing a grocery shopping experience with no checkout lines. Your grocery shopping is monitored by cameras, machine learning and a smartphone app. When you leave the supermarket, you're automatically billed for your purchases by Amazon. There are no checkout lines, no cashiers. It's grocery shopping ease through new Amazon technology which it's expected to rollout and expand in store operations in 2020. The base technology is Amazon Go.

Amazon Go
Amazon is a global retailing behemoth created by entrepreneurs Jeff Bezos and his mother, first to sell books. It's made Jeff Bezos, by expanding his retail lines way beyond books, into the #1 or #2 richest person in the world. It's only natural that Bezos would target grocery shopping through his proprietary online technology in a big way. It looks like he's ready to greatly grow his Amazon Go technology. Also, there are indications he's ready to open a brand new grocery chain brand, alongside of Whole Foods and his current 21 Amazon Go stores.

Cashier-Less, No Checkout Line Grocery Shopping
Amazon is poised to expand its Amazon Go technology of cashier-less grocery shopping that it has introduced in a small format at 21 stores. Amazon wants to expand the concept into full-scale supermarket size. In fact, they're testing it at a 10,400 sf. level in Seattle right now. Amazon wants to go to the traditional supermarket, 30,000 sf level.

2020 Plans
Amazon wants to open larger supermarket and smaller pop-up stores during the first quarter of 2020. It may even license its cashier-less technology to rival supermarkets, that are also experimenting with cashier-less checkouts.

Amazing Amazon Tech
Here's how Amazon's tech works. They're using in-store cameras and machine vision to track what customers are purchasing.

That combines with customers scanning an app onto their smartphone, that tracks in tandem with the store cameras, what the customer is putting in their cart. When the customer leaves the store, they're automatically billed for their purchases by Amazon. That sounds like a new way to shop for groceries.

46. Apple's Augmented Reality Headset and Glasses

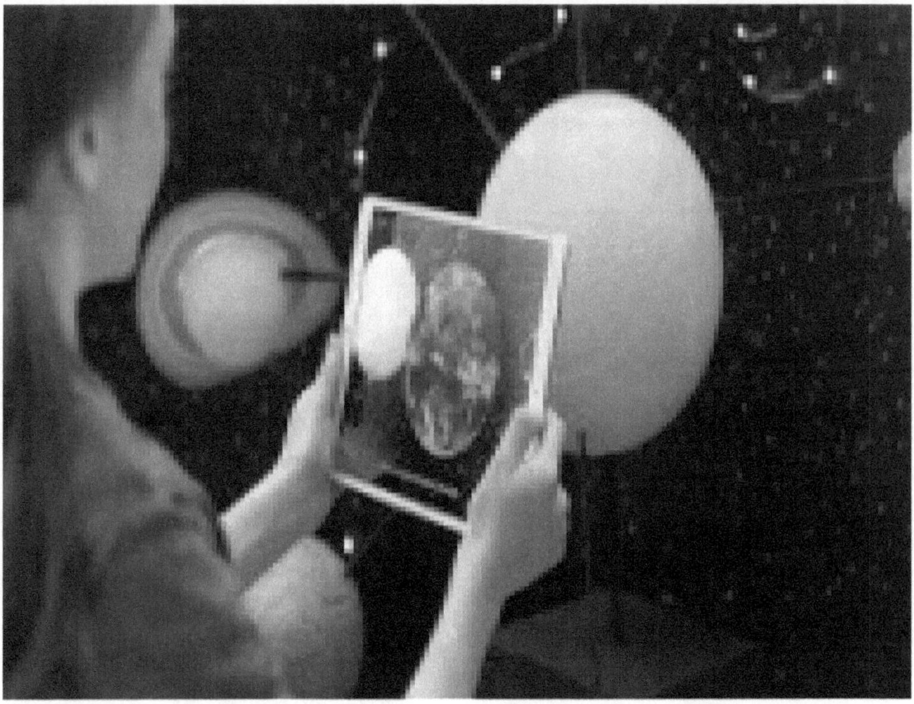

Source: Apple

2022 and 2023

Apple is looking to release an AR headset by 2022 and a sleek set of AR glasses by 2023. CEO Tim Cook believes AR technology will be potentially as important as the iPhone. Apple executives have briefed their employees on the plans.

New 3D Sensor Operating System

Reports indicate that Apple intends to use a 3D sensor system to support the AR headset and glasses. These systems would have the capability to create 3D reconstructions of objects, rooms and people. New, top of the line iPhones and a new iPad Pro could be available with the 3D sensor operating system sometime in 2020.

New Mixed Reality Systems
There are also indications that Apple engineers in the iPhone and iPad groups are working on a mixed reality headset and glasses operating system called rOS. No details from Apple on that intriguing technology.

47. China Is Officially Working on 6G Tech

Source: Stock Image of 6G

6G Tech is Faster than Fast
China has officially started researching and developing 6G technology. What is the potential of that kind of telecommunica-

tions? The potential is mobile networks that support 1 terabyte per second speeds. A huge leap in communications. This will be the next generation of cellular data services that will follow the emerging super-fast 5G tech systems.

China's Approach

China's approach is official and structured. Their purpose is to promote the latest wireless technology. Two offices have been created by the government of China to lead the effort. One office is comprised of Chinese government officials from agencies responsible for policy making. The second office is composed of their best experts from academia, think tanks and companies.

6G - The Sky is the Limit

Chinese government officials say 6G technology is in the exploratory phase. There is no consensus on its potentialities and applications. The Chinese say there is even no definition of 6G technology itself. But, clearly the sky is the limit on 6G tech. And the Chinese are applying a disciplined and structured approach to their R&D efforts.

48. China's Important Wearable Device Breakthrough

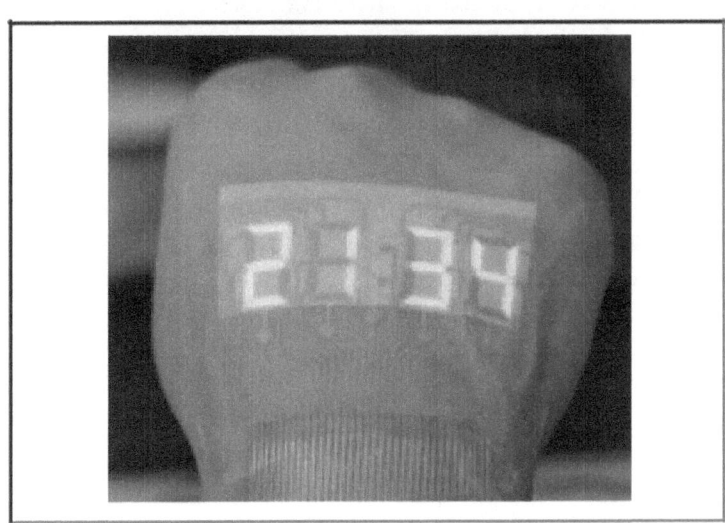

Source: Wrist Watch Bionic from Nanjing University

Safe, Low Power Display Screens on Your Skin

This is fascinating new innovation from Chinese researchers at Nanjing University. They've invented a new way to put displays like a wrist watch bionic or real time medical readouts on your skin. The extremely thin device is said to be safe, flexible and requires very little power to operate. It's a new wearable similar to a temporary tattoo but it displays electronic data like time.

Tech that Could Revolutionize Wearables

This new technology could revolutionize wearable devices for many users. For runners, it could mean a bionic watch taped on your hand to watch your times as you run. For health care tracking, it could mean real-time displays on your skin of medical data from already flexible medical devices.

What Makes This New

The Chinese researchers have overcome the need for high voltage to operate skin wearables, which can potentially hurt the user. They have also overcome power drainage problems. What makes their approach new is their device, which is a new type of stretchable, dielectric material, made of ceramic nanoparticles, along with silver nanowire electrodes and light emitting microparticles, all in a stretchy polymer. The screen they've invented can be seen indoors even in low voltage lighting. I first found this news in the American Chemical Society (ACS) Materials Letter. The ACS letter suggests this technology has a lot of potential including to be used by hospitals to display live health data readings on individual patients. Below is Nanjing University researchers' diagram of what they've invented.

49. Protecting Connected Vehicles from Hackers

Source: Upstream

Israel's Upstream Security Secures Millions in Funding

Israel's Upstream Security has secured $30 million in funding to develop software to protect connected and autonomous vehicles from cyberattacks by hackers. The funding is coming from automakers like Renault, Nissan, Mitsubishi, Hyundai and Volvo Truck, Nationwide Mutual Insurance and venture capital firms. Upstream takes a cloud based automotive cybersecurity approach using data analytics and machine learning algorithms. The company was established in 2017 and has received a total of $41 million in funding.

New Software Market with Exponential Growth

The market demand for software to protect against automotive cyberattacks is expected to reach $2.3 billion by 2025. The exponential growth is being driven by the fact that the more connectivity included in vehicles, the more vulnerable they are to hackers. Cyber carjacking has been an issue since 2015 when Wired magazine reported on researchers hacking a Jeep Cherokee vehicle while it was being driven. The objective now, including by Upstream Security, is to develop software that provides the strongest possible security to protect connected cars from hackers.

50. Apple's Next G, Health Tracking Smart Clothing

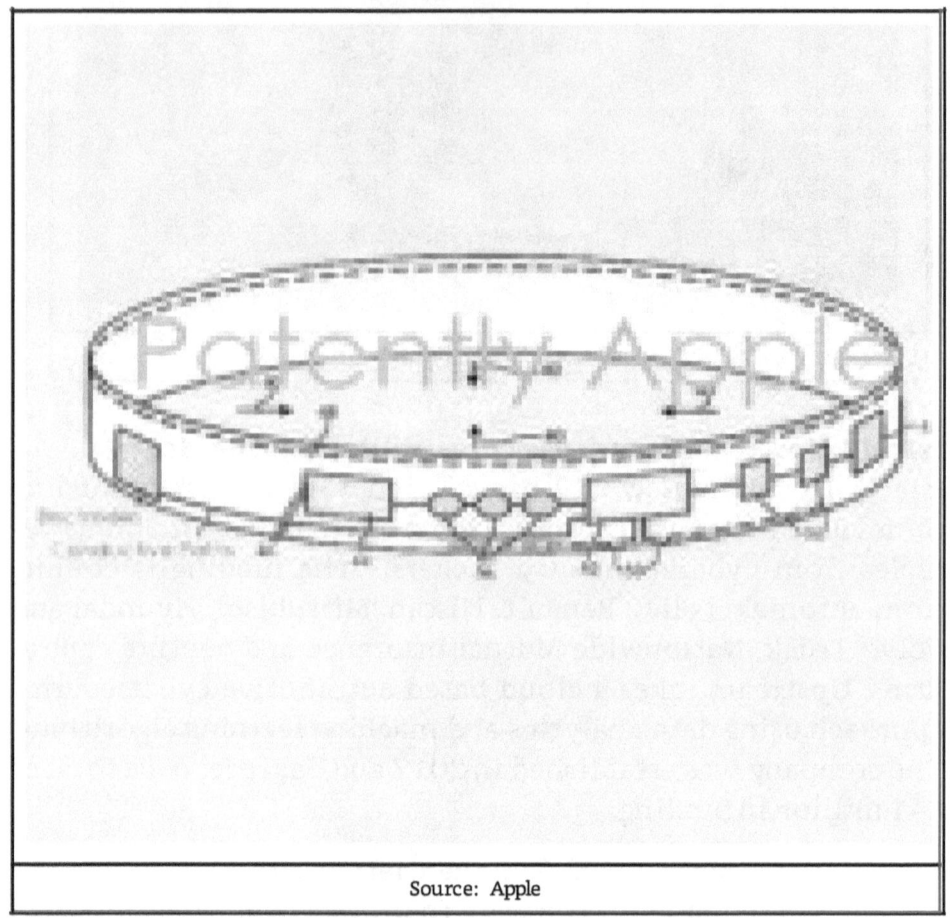

Source: Apple

Apple's Health Sensor Band

Apple has a new, patented idea. Health tracking sensors embedded by sewing them directly into clothing. Apple says this is beyond the Apple Watch. They're calling it the next generation of Smart Clothing with integrated circuitry, that is able to measure health data. They add it may work in concert with the Apple Watch to provide more accurate ECG readings.

Sensor Band that's Flexible

What Apple has patented is a soft elastic band with sensors to monitor heart rate, blood pressure, respiration and fitness related data. The type of stretchy material used is key to the design because the sensors need to be in constant contact with the body to get accurate readings.

Paired Device and Washable Band

The health measurement information would be transmitted wirelessly to a paired device to be read. And incredibly Apple says the health band device can be cleaned in a standard washing machine.

51. Smart Camera for Exercise at Home & Gym: GymCam

Source: Carnegie Mellon University

New Smart Camera, New Algorithm, New Exercise Tracking

Carnegie Mellon University engineers have developed a smart fitness tracker for the gym and for your home exercise area. The GymCam system scans the crowds in a gym to automatically identify exercises and count the number of repetitions. All that's needed is a stationary camera with the new algorithm in a gym to detect exercise, the type of exercise and reliably count the number of repetitions. In your home for personal use, it can do the same functions. It works with a smartphone for a person to record and track their workouts at home. CMU says a number of companies are expressing interest in the system for in-home exercise.

Vision Based System with New Algorithm

This is a vision based system that employs a new algorithm to detect repetitive motion. The CMU inventors say it goes beyond wearable sensors like smart watches, which they say don't track all exercises equally. The GymCam system operates with computer vision software. In a gym it communicates with your smartphone or can be paired with a piece of exercise equipment. It allows an athlete, in the gym or at home, to focus on the workout and not sweat the count.

52. Polaroid: Smart Phone Images to Instant Photos

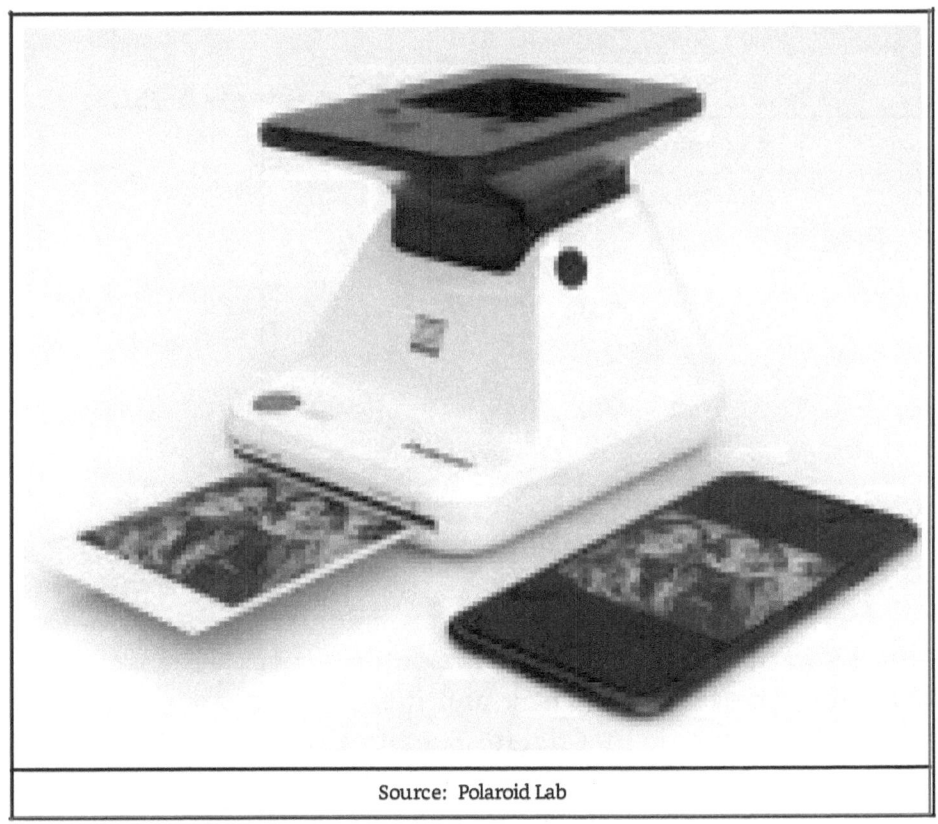

Source: Polaroid Lab

From the Cloud to the Real World

Polaroid Lab has invented a device that enables you to turn digital images from your smartphone to instant Polaroid photos. These are hard copy photos from digital images that you can put in a photo album or place on your fridge to remind you of the "Polaroid moment".

Elegantly Simple

The new device is simple to use. You select an image from your phone using a companion app. Then, you place the phone with the selected digital image face down on the Polaroid device. You push a button and with a combination of light, mirrors and Polaroid "chemistry" the system gives you an instant photo copy of the digital image. This takes your digital photos from the Cloud back to the real world as tangible photos.

53. Smart Connected Backpack from Google & YSL

Source: Yves Saint Laurent Smart Backpack

Smart Shoulder Strap Powered by Google Project Jacquard
It's called the Cit-E Backpack and it features a smart shoulder strap that's powered by Google. Specifically, by Google's Project Jacquard, an innovative concept that involves transforming ordinary objects like clothing and backpacks into interactive surfaces. It weaves touch and gestures into any textile to enable connectivity. The smart backpack is manufactured by Yves Saint Laurent in a partnership with Google. YSL is a fashion titan and the price is pricey at $878.

Smart Strap, Smart Phone
There's a tiny module containing a battery and hardware made by Google that fits into a hollowed-out space in the backpack's compartment. The module works with the wearer's cellphone and allows the left shoulder strap to control the phone. There's a special cell phone pocket inside the backpack.

Backpack with Connectivity
By the user's hand gestures like taps or swipes on the shoulder strap, the phone is controlled and takes commands. The wearer

can change the music or listen to messages. It's wearable connectivity.

54. New AR Headset From BAE That's Like Glasses

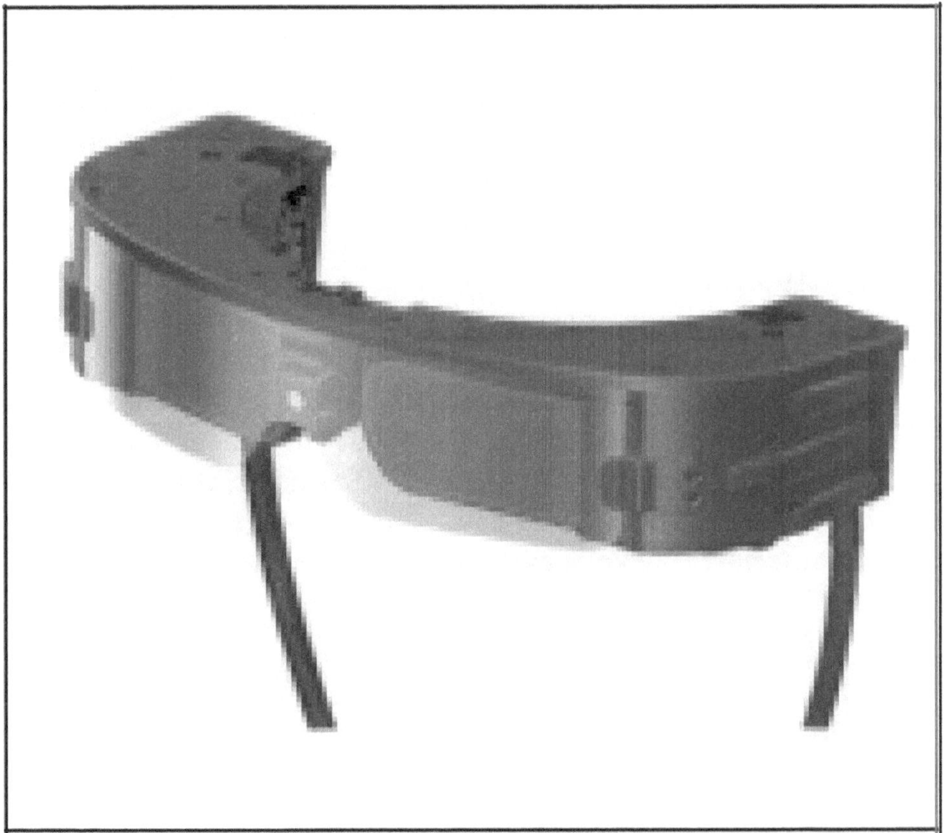

Source: BAE Systems

Designed with Extensive Input from Military and Commercial Users

BAE Systems' new augmented reality headset is designed for extended use and in rugged, harsh environments. The company says they've just put AR technology into a headset that's the size of a regular pair of eyeglasses. They've finalized a prototype that they believe brings the technology a lot closer to the highest performing, brightest and most durable AR glasses on the market today. Their technology has been developed with extensive input from military and commercial market users. It is advancing technology of importance to consumer markets.

Full Color, Wide Field of View Tech

This AR headset is specifically designed for military and defense end market users but it contains interesting tech that could find its way through adaptations into the consumer market. For instance, the AR glasses offer full color images and are light weight. There is a wide, 40 by 30 degree field of view. For the military, that provides a wide view of situational awareness.

Military Applications

For the military, which is targeted for first use, this AR tech is awesome. Just for the Navy, it enables officers to view ship operations while not in the operational control center or on the bridge. It has an advanced head-tracking system that ensures maps are accurately overlaid on the real world. For users, there is an important personal detail. The headset has a compact and well-balanced frame, just like your eye glasses.

55. Google Tech Gets Big Win from GM

Source: GM

Embedding Google Tech in 3.6 Million Cars Yearly

GM has selected Google Technology, parent company Alphabet, to be embedded in their vehicles starting in 2021. The win for Google is huge. Their tech could be installed in 3.6 million GM vehicles yearly. The Google technology will power navigation and provide voice-activated controls. It will also deliver expanded infotainment functions. Google beat Amazon for this deal which is part of a big, emerging race among technology companies to control vehicle dashboards, globally.

Google Apps Onboard GM Vehicles

Google Assistant, Google Maps and other applications will be available through the Google Play App Store for all GM brands. The first brands with built-in Google technology will roll in 2021 with more to come. The one market this won't be immediately available in is China.

Amazon Verses Google

This Google win was a big defeat for Amazon which is trying to sell its rival and very popular Alexa voice assistant technology to global automakers. GM says it will disclose the pricing of this new embedded Google technology closer to launch in 2021.

56. Bosch's Light Drive, Smart Connected Glasses

Source: Bosch

Next-G of Smartglasses

This new innovation in eyewear from Bosch Sensortec lets you stay focused with your prescription eye glasses and stay connected for your calls, email messages, navigation alerts and a lot more. Bosch has designed these glasses to be totally conventional looking, like any other normal pair of glasses. But these glasses are far from conventional and normal. They are a first in all-day transparency to deliver high quality, bright images through connectivity. Bosch says it eliminates the need to check any messages from mobile devices. The glasses pull it all in and display it for you. Bosch calls it an all-day wearable.

Bosch at CES 2020

The Bosch Sensortec team's Light Drive glasses are stylish, lightweight and loaded with HUD tech. The tech behind the glasses is extraordinary. They rely on a microelectromechanical scanner. The device scans onto a holographic element in the lens. It redirects light onto the retina of the wearer. The result is a clear display of information like e-messages.

Extraordinary Tech

This type of wearable tech is extraordinary. The system incorporates MEMS mirrors, optical elements, sensors and onboard processing. It pairs with connected smartphones and other devices. It works even in bright, direct sunlight. And it can even display your To-Do shopping list.

SECTION FIVE: ENVIRONMENTAL & ENERGY INNOVATIONS

57. Wearable Solar Panels

SunUp
This is a wearable solar panel called SunUp for easy use to travel with you and recharge a battery by solar power. Possible uses include using the flexible device to fit around your backpack as you walk to University. It can also fit around your tent and pick up solar rays while you are on a forest adventure. You can even use it on your kayak to pull in solar rays as you enjoy the beauty of water sporting. This device can pull in 15 watts to fully charge a mobile device within 12 hours. It's a new piece of charging up while enjoying the environment by the green, clean energy of the sun.

Top Recognized Tech
This device is a national top runner up at the James Dyson new innovation awards. It was created by Brunel University design

student Bradley Brister. It overcomes many efficiency limits of existing technology by using triangles of polycrystalline panels to increase efficiency.

58. MIT's New System to Fight Climate Change

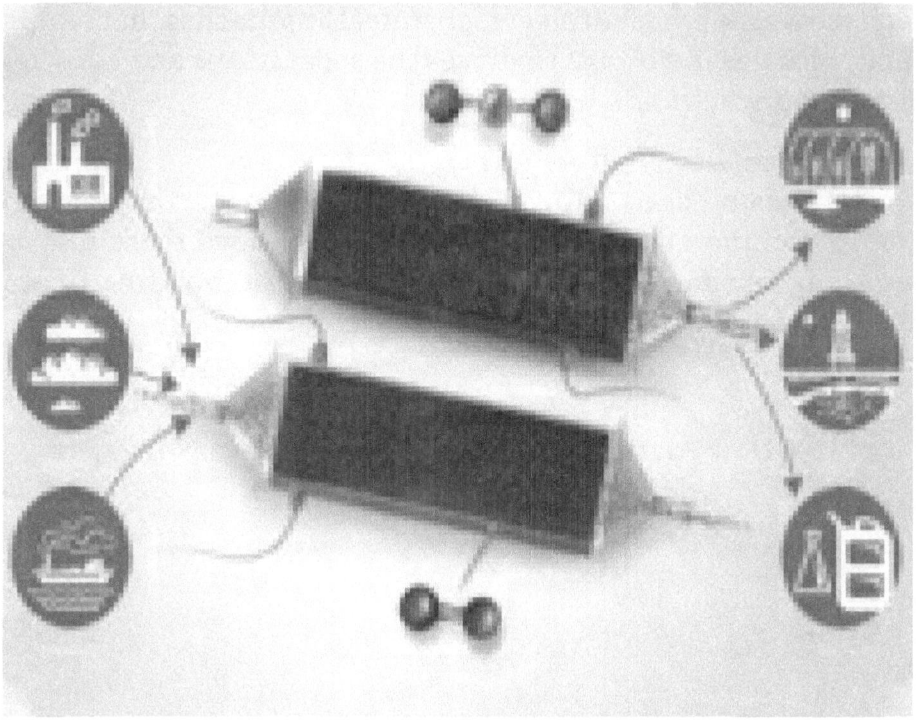

Source: MIT image of the system

New Carbon Capture Technology from MIT Engineers

This new technology is from MIT engineers to clean the air of CO_2 and fight climate change. Their invention removes CO_2 from air streams at almost any concentration levels, from the open air to emissions from power plants. MIT says it works like a large battery and it requires low energy and low money to operate when compared to other approaches.

Like a Battery

Like a very large battery, the MIT system absorbs CO2 from a gas stream that passes over its electrodes as it charges up. While going through the process, the device alternates between charging and discharging. During the charging cycle, fresh air blows through the system. During discharging, concentrated carbon dioxide blows through. As the process is done, pure carbon dioxide is discharged. The MIT engineers say their carbon capture tech shows the power of electrochemical approaches that require small changes in voltage to drive "the separations and blow out pure carbon dioxide".

New Company
The MIT team has developed and launched a new company Verdox to commercialize the system. They believe there may be some big initial applications, such as for the bottling of soft drinks and creating plant-based fuel alternatives.

59. New Portable, Air Quality Monitor from Singapore

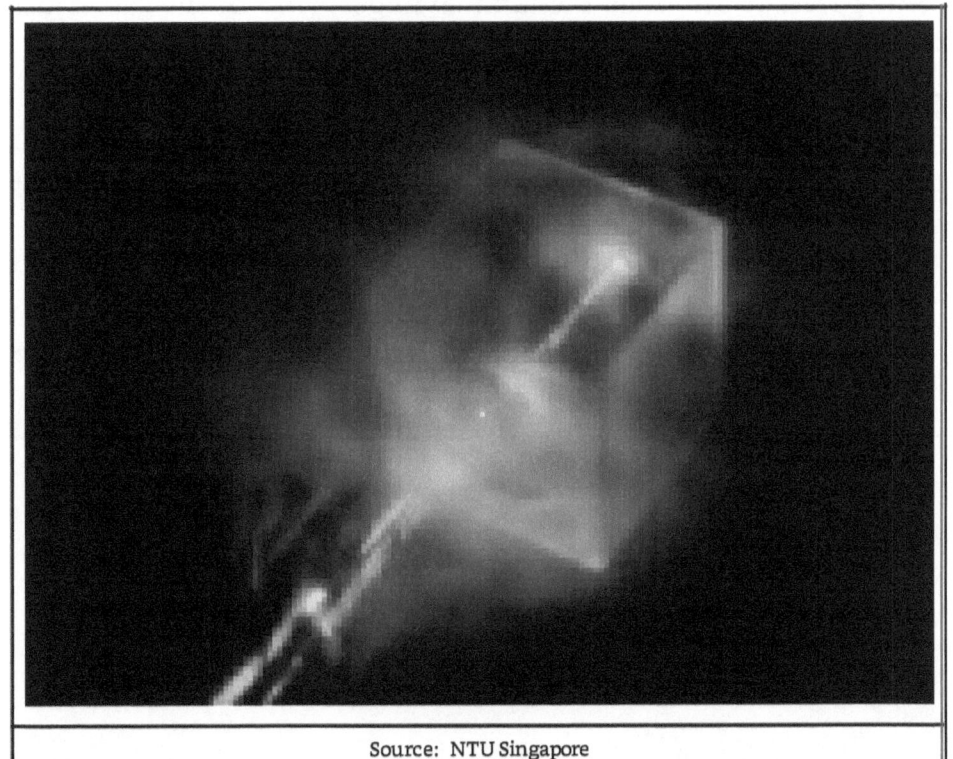

Source: NTU Singapore

Real-Time Detection of Toxic Gases & Chemicals in the Air

Researchers at Nanyang Technological University - NTU Singapore - have invented a sensor that can identify a wide range of airborne gases and chemicals instantly. This includes gas leaks and pollution toxins both indoors and outside. The prototype device is portable and made for rapid deployment by agencies to identify airborne hazards immediately.

Seconds Fast Results

Current technology can require up to a few days to identify specific toxins in the air. This new sensor is made for emergency situations that require quick and ongoing analysis. The device is composed of a chip made from a porous nanomaterial that traps gas particles. A laser beamed on the chip interacts with the gas molecules to produce a lower energy light. That light is analyzed by a camera to see if its spectroscopic signature matches known toxic gases. It provides a "chemical fingerprint" of the gas in just ten seconds, not days.

Camera Analysis Can Be in Remote Location
Importantly, the camera analysis can be done at a distance, keeping the responders in a safer location. This new, innovative sensor technology was invented by scientists at NTU Singapore.

60. From The Netherlands: Drone Performs R/T Water Quality Tests

Source: Pelican Drone, TU Delft

Water Testing in Minutes
The Pelican amphibious drone is able to deliver water tests in

minutes. This new technology is game-changing because current water quality testing is time and labor intensive, requires on site visits by humans and then the water samples have to be transported to a lab. The traditional process is expensive and many times the water samples no longer accurately reflect current water conditions, which dynamically change. The Pelican drone provides water quality testing results in real-time.

Autonomous and Real Time Water Monitoring
A team at Delft University of Technology in The Netherlands has invented the Pelican drone that flies over the water surface and scans it for problem areas with its onboard hyperspectral cameras. If there's a potential problem, the drone swoops down and takes a water sample. The sample is transferred to a portable cytasense flow cytometer, which is a water testing measuring instrument. The results are given in minutes.

Pelican Drone Diver
The Pelican drone is much faster and more efficient than traditional methods of checking for water quality issues like blue-green algae. It's able to monitor water quality autonomously and in real-time. The TU Delft researchers are developing the drone to not only land on the water surface but to dive underwater automatically. The companion measuring instrument is capable of scanning and analyzing tens of thousands of microorganisms and photographing thousands in a few minutes. This very quick process revolutionizes monitoring water quality and prevents deterioration of water testing samples for much more accurate reads.

61. Ocean Wave-Solar Renewable Energy System

Source: EcoWave Power

World's 1st Grid Connected Wave Energy Array

The EcoWave Power is a world first. The Swedish invention converts both wave and solar power into green renewable energy on the same device. It's deployed in the port city of Jaffa, Israel and is connected to the city's electric grid. This is the world's only grid connected wave energy array. The device is also topped with solar panels to generate more energy. The innovative technology consists of floaters on coastal waters attached to existing man-made structures. This makes the system accessible and simple to install and maintain. The additional solar panel components are deployed and being tested in Jaffa.

Wave+Solar Power Generation Provides Many Benefits

The system converts the rise and fall of coastal water into electricity and has worked effectively for several years. To increase efficiency, the Swedish team added solar panels on top of the floating green energy generation system already deployed on the water. There are many benefits, including increased energy production, no extra land use needed and the cooling water around the solar panels reduces energy loss from heat.

New Energy Innovation Making a Difference for the Environment
EcoWave Power is headquartered in Stockholm. They are developing new energy innovation targeted at making a difference for the environment.

62. **Combating Climate Change: New Bioreactor More Effective Than 400 Trees**

Source: Hypergiant Industries

Converts CO2 into Biofuel

This is breakthrough new energy innovation to combat Climate Change. The Eos Bioreactor pulls carbon dioxide from the atmosphere with greater efficiency than 400 trees. The footprint is only 3x3x7 feet. The creator is Hypergiant Industries of Texas.

Algae & Tubes

The machine is filled with tubes that contain algae. The algae type chlorella vulgaris is able to absorb more CO2 than any other plant. The algae consume the CO2 and converts it into biofuels that can be harvested. There's a great deal of intelligence behind the process.

Artificial and Machine Intelligence

Hypergiant Industries say their Eos Bioreactor is more efficient than trees - 400 times more effective in pulling out CO2 from the air in the same unit area. They use artificial and machine intelligence to constantly monitor and manage air flow, amount, type of light, temperature, ph, biodensity and other factors to maintain maximum carbon sequestration.

63. New, Transformative Device to Generate Power from Night Sky

Source: UCLA

Renewable and Complements Solar Power

This new, inexpensive thermoelectric device may be transformative in energy generation. It harvests the coldness of space during the night to generate electricity - enough right now to power a LED light at nighttime, but the inventors say it's very scalable. The device is a significant new innovation from engineers at UCLA and Stanford University. The gadget works at night when solar systems don't. The inventors say it's a new approach to power generation when power at night is needed. It complements solar power that doesn't work at night, giving a 24/7 approach to green, renewable energy.

Phenomenon Like Frost Formation

The device takes advantage of radiative cooling, the process by which frost forms on grass during above freezing temperatures at night. The sky facing surface of the technology passes heat to the atmosphere as thermal radiation. It loses some heat to space and reaches a temperature cooler than the surrounding air. That temperature differential produces renewable energy at night, when lighting demands are peak.

Scalable Tech for Global Use

According to the UCLA and Stanford engineers, their invention is highly scalable. The radiative cooling device essentially consists of an aluminum disk coated with paint and all the other components are readily available for purchase off the shelf. This is important innovation to watch for because of its practicality and scalability for worldwide use to supplement solar energy at night.

64. Microwave Sized Water Harvester from UC Berkeley

Source: UC Berkeley's Water Harvester

Capable of Supplying Fresh Water to Global Villages in Need
One of humanity's biggest challenges is to develop technology to meet global drinking water supply needs. A team at UC Berkeley has invented a new water harvester capable of collecting water from very dry desert air. Most importantly, the team says their technology is scalable and capable of supplying clean drinking water to people in villages. This technology promises to be a new source of clean drinking water to people in arid environments globally.

New Engineering
The device has been tested in the Mojave Desert and it works. The base is a metal-organic framework (MOF) that pulls in and condenses water molecules from the very dry desert air. The cartridges of MOFs are in a large, transparent box that includes a condenser to collect the water molecules as liquid water.

Third Variation on an Innovative Theme
This is UC Berkeley's third version of the device. They've increased its efficiency by ten-times by using a solar-powered fan and heat to increase water collection. The device is microwave sized and can harvest five cups of water a day. But the big deal is this technology can be scaled- up to supply the daily clean, drinkable water needs of small villages and perhaps beyond.

65. New Tech for Ocean Plastic Clean-Ups

Ocean Cleanup Source:

Pacific Garbage Patch Success from Ocean Cleanup

Ocean Cleanup is a foundation, headquartered in Rotterdam, The Netherlands, that develops advanced systems to rid the world's oceans of plastics. They've reported the successful use of parachute-like devices as part of their Ocean Project System 001B in the Pacific's so-called Garbage Patch to aggressively capture ocean plastic pollution and it worked brilliantly. 001B is a highly advanced barrier system to retrieve the global dumping of plastics in the oceans. The addition of the parachute-like device enhanced the capture of ocean plastic into the barrier.

Parachute-Like Devices Attached to Barrier Worked Beautifully

The Pacific Garbage Patch, loaded with plastic pollution that gets worse environmentally daily, is three times the size of France and twice the size of Texas. Floating plastic is light, fast moving and difficult to contain on the ocean. The floating speed of plastic makes it difficult for humans to recover it. By attaching the parachute-like device to the organization's barrier, the system slowed down the fast moving plastic enough to make it go through the opening of the barrier and capture it.

Sea Trials and Projected Results
The parachute addition to the Ocean Cleanup System 001B system worked so well that it hit the overflow plastic retrieval line and has caused the team to increase the system's diameter for upcoming sea trials. They think their passive drift system can clean up half of the Pacific Garbage Patch within five years.

Young Entrepreneur and Inventor Behind This Innovation
The founder of Ocean Cleanup is Dutch inventor and entrepreneur Boyan Slat who invents technologies to solve societal problems like global ocean plastic pollution. Boyan started this significant global foundation in 2013 at the age of 18 and it's been growing ever since.

66. SoftBank's Vision Fund Investing Big in Swiss Startup Energy Vault

Source: Solar Vault computer rendering

Storing Solar and Wind Energy for 24/7 Use

Switzerland's energy storage technology company Energy Vault has received a $110 million investment from SoftBank's Vision Fund, one of the world's largest technology investors. The company stores wind and solar energy in a huge tower of concrete blocks. It uses software to autonomously control the energy tower's operations including a 400 foot, 6 armed crane that stacks the energy storage blocks. And it uses algorithms to account for changes in energy supply and demand, weather, grid needs and other factors. Storing renewable energy is the biggest challenge facing the green energy industry. Energy Vault has a very innovative solution that SoftBank's Vision Fund is betting on.

Global Expansion

Energy Vault relies on low cost materials like cement blocks to provide energy storage. It says it's a much cheaper method than lithium-ion batteries to store electricity. The company says their technology enables renewables to deliver baseload power for a lower cost than fossil fuels 24/7. Through storage, the system eliminates the intermittent and unpredictable nature of wind and solar power. With the Japanese Vision Fund investment, Energy Vault will deploy its technology globally, starting with large-scale prototype plants in Italy and India.

67. Passive Cooling: Staying Cool with No Electricity Or Batteries

Source: University of Buffalo

New Innovation Incorporating Solar Energy and Outer Space

This is new energy innovation from engineers at the University of Buffalo. A green, renewable way to keep buildings cool in urban areas. It's a passive cooling system that absorbs heat and beams it as heat radiation to outer space, while keeping the environment around the system cool. What's remarkable, this system is self-sustaining and requires no electricity or batteries to power it.

Unique and Inexpensive

The device consists of an inexpensive film composed of polymer/aluminum that is put in a box inside of what the engineers call a "solar shelter" that they also invented. The special film absorbs the heat from the air and keeps the surroundings cool. The solar shelter serves two purposes: blocking incoming sunlight and beaming the heat into space through a narrow beam passageway as thermal radiation. The team says that narrow heat radiation passageway is also unique to their system.

Crowded Cities with High Rise Buildings
The narrow beam of heat radiation speeding to space that the system has uniquely created is very important to crowded urban areas surrounded by high rise buildings. It potentially provides a heat thruway to space in crowded places and provides "air conditioned" buildings. To cool a building, numerous units of the system would be needed to cover the roof. The team's landmark research results were published in Nature Sustainability.

SECTION SIX: TRAVEL INNOVATION

68. GM's Steering Wheel-Less Cars

Source: GM CEO Mary Barra with Cruise Autonomous Car

Computers in the Driver's Seat

GM is engaged in talks with the US National Highway Safety Administration (NHSA) to secure permission to deploy a limited number of steering wheel-less, fully autonomous cars on US roads. The cars are designed to be totally autonomous with no steering wheel and no human controls. Essentially, computers are in the driver's seat. GM believes this could make for safer driving and less accidents. The head of the NHSA has confirmed that the Agency is doing due diligence on the GM request.

New Automated Piloting Systems

The federal agency expects to make a decision on the request sometime in 2020. It also will make a judgement on a petition by the driverless delivery service Nuro to deploy a limited number of low-speed, delivery trucks with no humans onboard. These highly automated piloting systems for road vehicles and also for airplanes have the potential of revolutionizing air and ground transportation. The NHSA says that it understands the important, precedent-setting nature of its decision on both requests.

GM's Autonomous and Electric Priorities

GM and Nuro are among the leading transportation companies pushing the frontiers of driverless travel. For GM CEO Mary Barra, the development of autonomous and electric vehicles are two of her top priorities. The NHSA is pouring through the details to make sure the vehicles are as safe as cars driven by humans on the roads.

69. URBY: New Form of Electric Urban Transportation

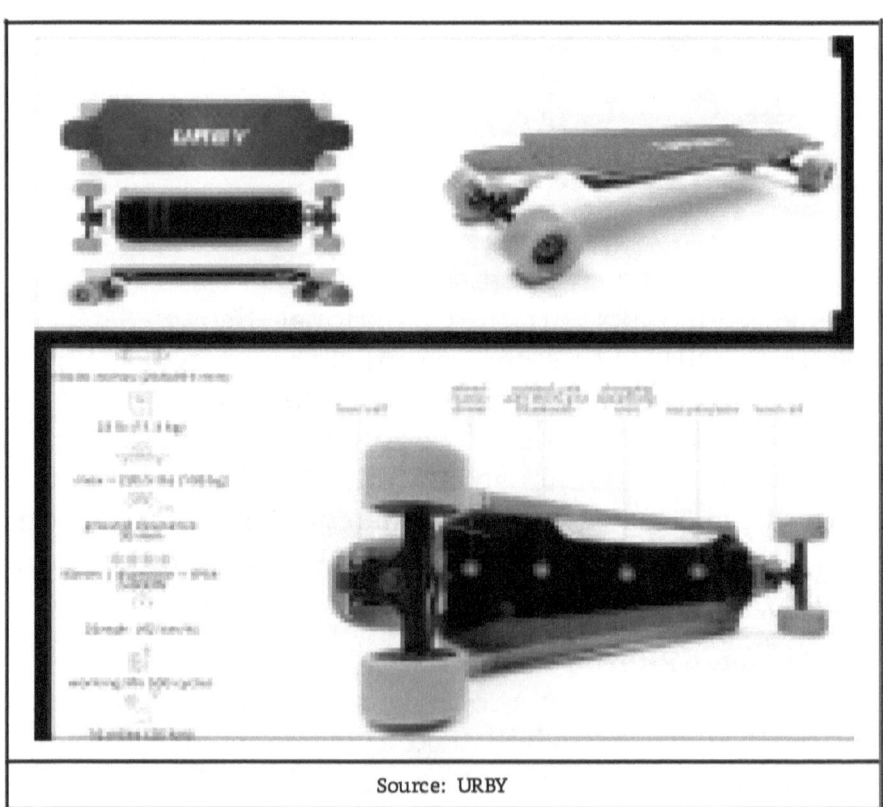

Source: URBY

Electric Longboards - Personal Mobility

This new, electric travel technology could radically change your city commute. URBY is an electric, hands-free skateboard. It's the next generation of smart, powerful electric longboards that are loaded with technology.

URBY

The all-electric board is 10x36 inches, weighs 25 pounds, reaches maximum speeds of 26 mph and has a 16 mile range. The board is loaded with load cells that understand the movement of the center of gravity on the board as you coast along. According to the inventors, the board has a highly "intellectual" electric drive and maintains control through an intuitive interface for moving body weight. It's lighter and smaller than a bike or scooter and is eco-friendly as it is all-electric.

Kickstarter Investment Stage

URBY is available on Kickstarter . The electric longboard has an easy stop and go mechanism. There is no remote control. It has a mobile app to chronicle the right boarding mode and the parameters of the board for the individual rider. Besides app control, it has analytics. The control unit has both WIFI and Bluetooth. Marketed as "Individual Urban Transport", URBY has a futuristic design, 250Wh battery with the capacity for 500 rides. It's a green, clean, electric means to scoot around town.

70. For Electric Motorcycles, Solar Power

Source: Motosola

Solar Biking

The Motosola solar canopy mounted on top of an electric motor-cycle charges the battery of an electric bike by solar energy. In Asia, canopies on bikes are common to protect the riders from the sun. Motosola has taken that concept to a new level by inventing a canopy that's essentially a solar panel to pull in and utilize the energy of the sun to charge electric vehicles. The system consists of the canopy and a charge inverter. It's available as a 100 W or 150 W system. The company's prototype system in Shenzhen, China has been driven during the last quarter of 2019 without needing any recharge. The solar system has been sufficient to keep the batteries charged.

Green, Clean Biking

The company says that the system can generate up to 1.5kWh of electricity per day whether the bike is being ridden or it's parked.

It's said to be easy to install and compatible with most motor-bikes. When parked, the canopy can be tilted to a 45 degree angle for maximum solar energy absorption. The company says the solar awning can be adapted to a range of electric vehicles including e-scooters and e-bikes.

71. Revolutionary New Electric, Self-Heating Battery

Source: Penn State University

Recharges in 10 Minutes with Up to 300 Mile Range

The future of driving green and emissions free is electric. Now a team of engineers at Penn State University has invented a new battery to make that future a lot closer and more doable. Their new lithium-ion battery can be charged in ten minutes, self-heats and provides a driving range up to 300 miles. They envision this being done at local service stations with electric charges for EV's.

Revolutionary New Tech

This new battery is revolutionary. It can be recharged over and over again for up to 500,000 miles of travel. That's a big deal. Some lithium-ion batteries rapidly degrade based on ambient temperatures. This battery overcomes current limitations. The Penn State team has installed nickel foil on the batteries, eliminating lithium plating. The nickel warms quickly through resistance to 140F. That triggers rapid charging bursts of 10 minutes at a time and a ride of up to 300 miles that's all electric.

Future of Electric Driving

Fast charging and longer range driving are the keys to widespread use of electric cars. This is a charge in the right direction from Penn State engineers who are developing it. It's worth watching. The research was supported in part by the US Department of Energy.

72. Smart Wipers: Far Better Mapping of Wet Road Conditions

Source: Toyota

Toyota's New Tech Innovation

Toyota's connected windshield wipers are designed to create far more accurate weather maps when the wipers are operating. They're part of a joint project between Toyota and Japan-based Weathernews, which offers app based weather reports. The 2 companies conducted what they call a "verification test" using wiper data to provide drivers with real-time information about road weather risks. They say the tech is designed to increase driver safety by increasing the accuracy of available weather forecasts and data.

Lots of Tech Involved

The system uses the onboard loT communications in most new Toyota models, along with Big Data and artificial intelligence. It can detect whether wipers are on or off in designated regions. By using data on the operational status of wipers, Weathernews weather data and vehicle data from Toyota's connected vehicles, the system provides more accurate rain maps on road conditions and their surrounding areas.

Higher Accident Rates During Rainy Conditions
Accident rates during rain storms are four times higher than that of sunny days. The raincloud radar, that is typically used to forecast, can be porous and inaccurate when the rainclouds are in the lower levels of the atmosphere. Toyota's smart connected wipers, using AI, Big Data and connectivity, promise to deliver real-time warnings on wet weather making driving difficult.

73. MIT's ShadowCam – Making Autonomous Cars Safer

Source: MIT

Cars That See Around Corners

MIT engineers and computer scientists have invented a new de-vice - ShadowCam - that enables autonomous cars to see around corners and into shadows. The purpose is to help make self-driving cars safer and prevent accidents. By sensing tiny changes in shadows on the ground, the new system identifies approaching objects, such as cars and people that could cause an accident. It can detect a moving vehicle or person walking behind a pillar in a parking garage.

Advanced Warning System

The technology uses overlays of images that enable the car to identify shadows in real time and determine the direction of the object casting the shadows. Based on the information and analysis, the system tells the car to slow or stop. It is an advanced early warning system to prevent collisions.

Faster and Better than LiDAR

The MIT team is led by Prof. Daniela Rus, Director of CSAIL, MIT's Computer Science Artificial Intelligence Lab. Dr. Rus says their new tech beats traditional LiDAR, which can only detect visible objects, by a half second. The researchers add fractions of seconds matter with fast moving autonomous vehicles. ShadowCam has been tested indoors in enclosed parking lots. Their goal is to provide "X-ray vision" to self-driving cars on the streets and highways. The team adds that in the future service robots, delivering medicine and supplies in hospital hallways, could use the system to avoid colliding with people.

74. Gulfstream G700: Next G of Business/Private Jets

Source: Gulfstream

Flying Long Distance at Close to Mach 1

Gulfstream Aerospace, a unit of General Dynamics, unveiled its long anticipated G700 business jet at the world's largest corporate jet airshow in Las Vegas. Gulfstream says the G700 is a long range, enhanced speed and performance aircraft that is meant to set a new standard in long range business jets. According to Gulfstream President Mark Burns, it's an all new, advanced technology aircraft that "redefines safety, comfort and range at speed".

Delivered to Buyers in 2022
The G700 is priced at $75 million, powered by Rolls-Royce engines and has the tallest, longest and widest cabin in the business jet industry. It seats 19 passengers. This plane is built for distance, speed and comfort. It can fly 7500 nautical miles at Mach 0.85. It has five living areas, a 6-place dining or conference room, an extra large, ultra-galley with passenger lounge or crew compartments and a master suite with showers.

Turbulent Buying Times
These are turbulent buying times for the business/private jet industry against a backdrop of a slowing global economy, Brexit questions and US-China trade tensions, all of which are putting a down-draft on the corporate jet market. But global companies want larger corporate jets that fly greater distances and provide long haul travel. That's just what Gulfstream's G700 seems to be delivering.

75. Your Autonomous Mobility Future

Source: BMW Blog - Car2Go

Car2Go Driving FAS

Two global luxury brands are leading the way on new, automotive mobility for drivers. BMW and Daimler announced FAS. It's a 50-50 collaboration of Daimler's Car2Go car sharing business with BMW's DriveNow, ParkNow and e-ChargeNow. This is a burgeoning space for the automotive industry, a menu of new car sharing, parking and electric car recharging services. These mobility services could prove to be the ultimate and most important on the ground driving services for consumers before the era of flying vehicles takes-off by the mid 2020's.

FAS Forward

FAS is designed to give customers a wide choice across brands for the new menu of services. Daimler and BMW are looking for collaborators as well as financial investments in the new venture. The personal mobility space is just starting to accelerate. These ventures are more traditional, drive on the ground for now and include car sharing, parking and electric vehicle recharging services. The offer for new partners on FAS comes from the new BMW CEO Oliver Zipse today in a Frankfurt newspaper. He has an intuitive vision of the future of driving, right now, right on the road.

76. Porsche Invests in Advanced Systems for Road Visibility

Source: TriEye

Clearly Seeing the Road in the Worst Driving Conditions

Israeli startup TriEye has invented short wave, infrared sensing technology that enables unprecedented vision under the worst weather and night driving conditions. The company has expanded its funding round to $19 million with an investment from the German sports car manufacturer Porsche.

HD Cameras

TriEye's HD SWIR camera is smaller, has a higher resolution and costs "a fraction of the price", according to the company, of existing technologies. It has also been proven to work and is ready for mass production. The company says it will use the investment money for further product development and to build their team.

2020 Vision

The company's first cameras will launch in 2020. They will enable advanced driver assistance systems to achieve "unprecedented vision capabilities" under tough driving conditions like fog, bad weather and darkness. Porsche says it sees great potential in sensor technology for the next generation of driver assistance systems and autonomous driving systems.

77. Segway-Ninebot E-Scooter Innovation

Source: Segway-Ninebot's New Scooter in Beijing

Boon for the Scooter-Sharing Market

China's Segway-Ninebot, an electric scooter manufacturer, has a new piece of innovation. A scooter that can drive itself back to its charging station with no human onboard. This could prove to be a boon for the growing scooter-sharing industry, which is booming in big city, heavy traffic areas globally. Ride sharing companies like Uber and Lyft have expanded their business into the lucrative scooter-sharing market.

Self-Returning Scooters

Segway-Ninebot's new scooter is semi-autonomous, has three wheels, electric power and is able to drive itself back to its base charging station when someone's ride time has expired. This self-return feature could save companies like Lyft and Uber a lot of time and money. Up until now, the scooter ride sharing companies have generally dispatched paid employees to fetch the scooters and give them a recharge for the next rider. The next new innovation for scooters beyond self-returning is self-charging.

78. Elon Musk's Las Vegas Tunnel to Open in 2020

Source: The Boring Company

Musk's Boring Company that's Not so Boring

The first commercial version of Elon Musk's people mover tunnel will open in Las Vegas in 2020. It is designed as a "traffic busting" alternative to congested streets in crowded cities. The tunnel is one mile long. Musk announced that he expects the tunnel to open during 2020.

Las Vegas on the Move
The tunnel is being built by Musk's not-so-boring Boring Company. It connects the Las Vegas Convention Center to the Vegas Strip. The sprawling Convention Center is being enlarged and the tunnel is expected to facilitate traffic at the Center to the Strip where many of the city's major hotels and casinos are located.

Twin Tunnels
The Boring Company was commissioned by Las Vegas officials in spring 2019 to design, build and manage the twin tunnel system. Passengers will be transported in small autonomous vehicles carrying 8 to 16 people.

Travel Visionary
Musk is a visionary engineer who wants to revolutionize travel through his three major companies: Tesla, SpaceX and Boring. He's pushing for an underground train-like system called The Hyperloop. The Hyperloop would carry passengers in capsules through pressurized tubes at high speeds. He's built a test tunnel at one of his facilities in California.